ABSTRACT HARMONY: A COLORING JOURNEY"

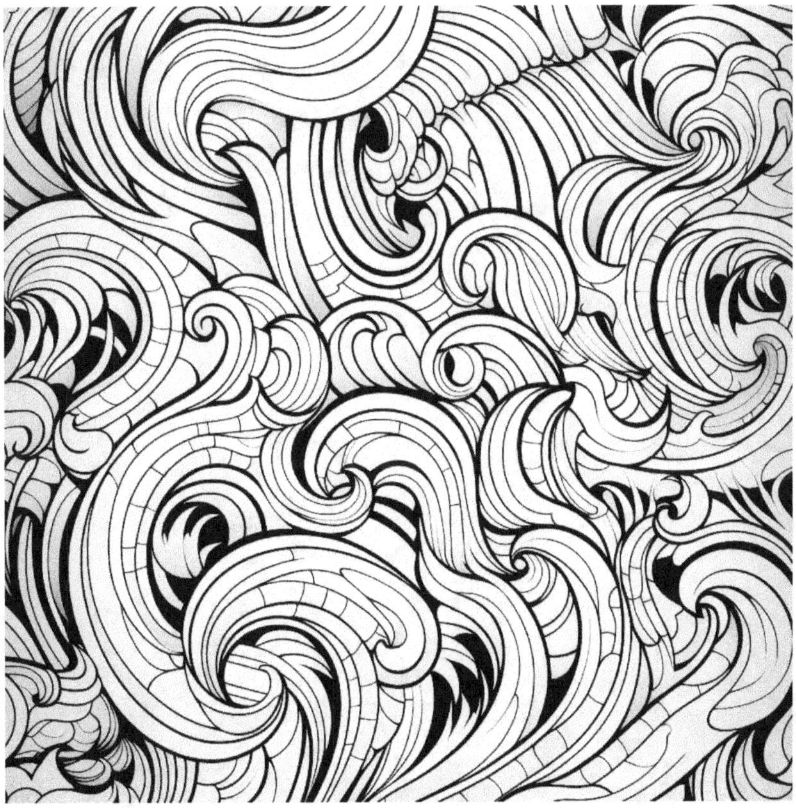

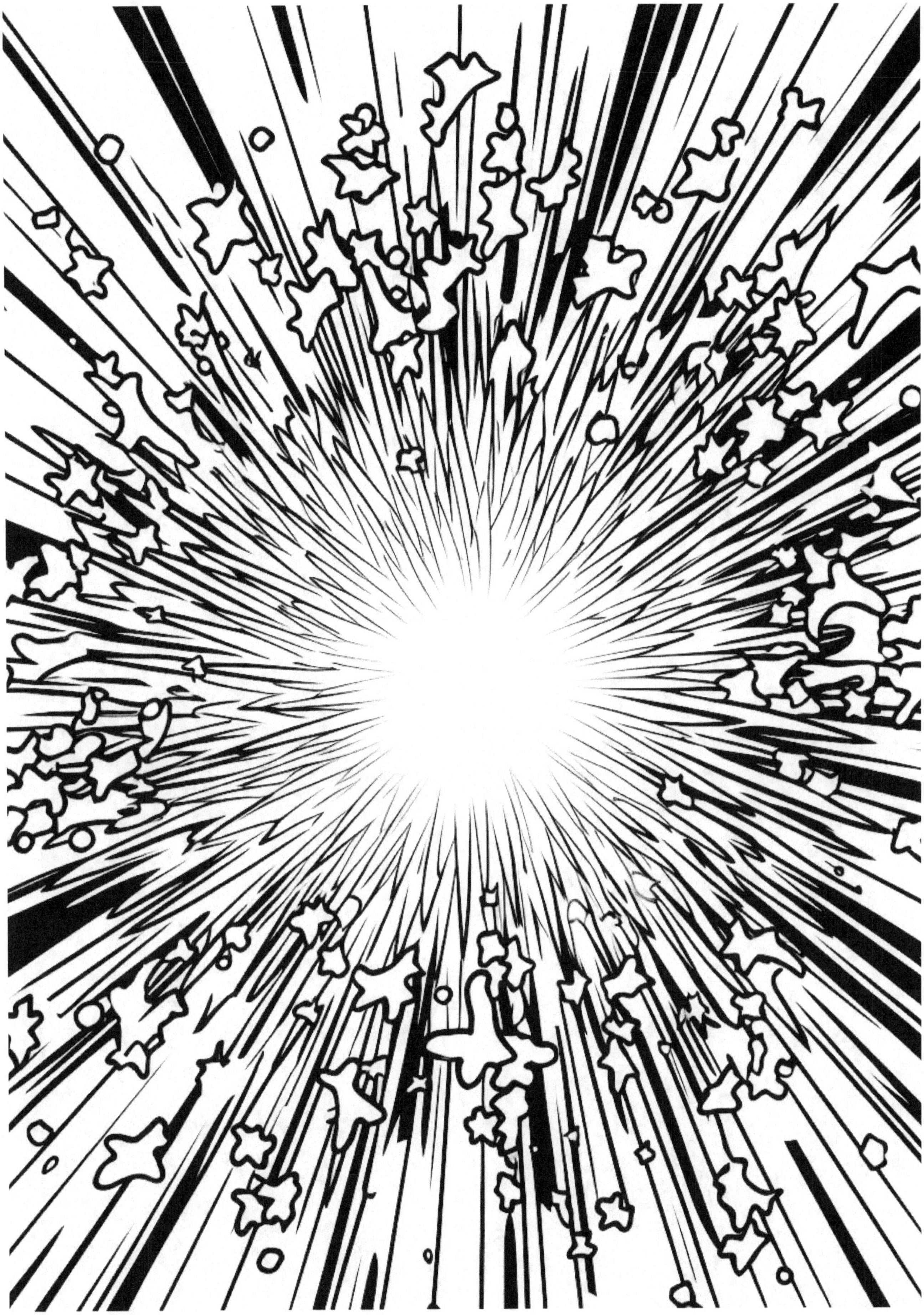

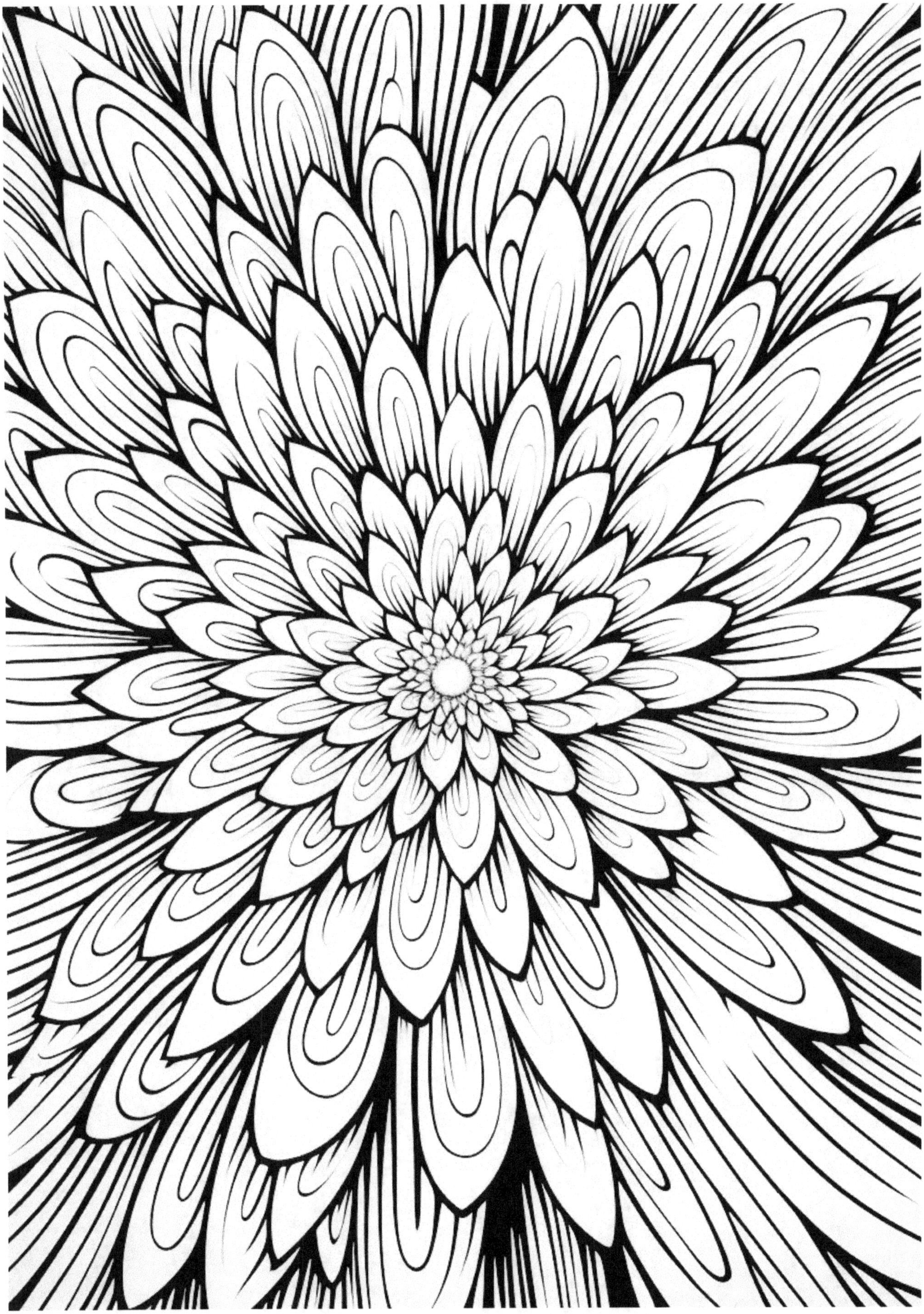

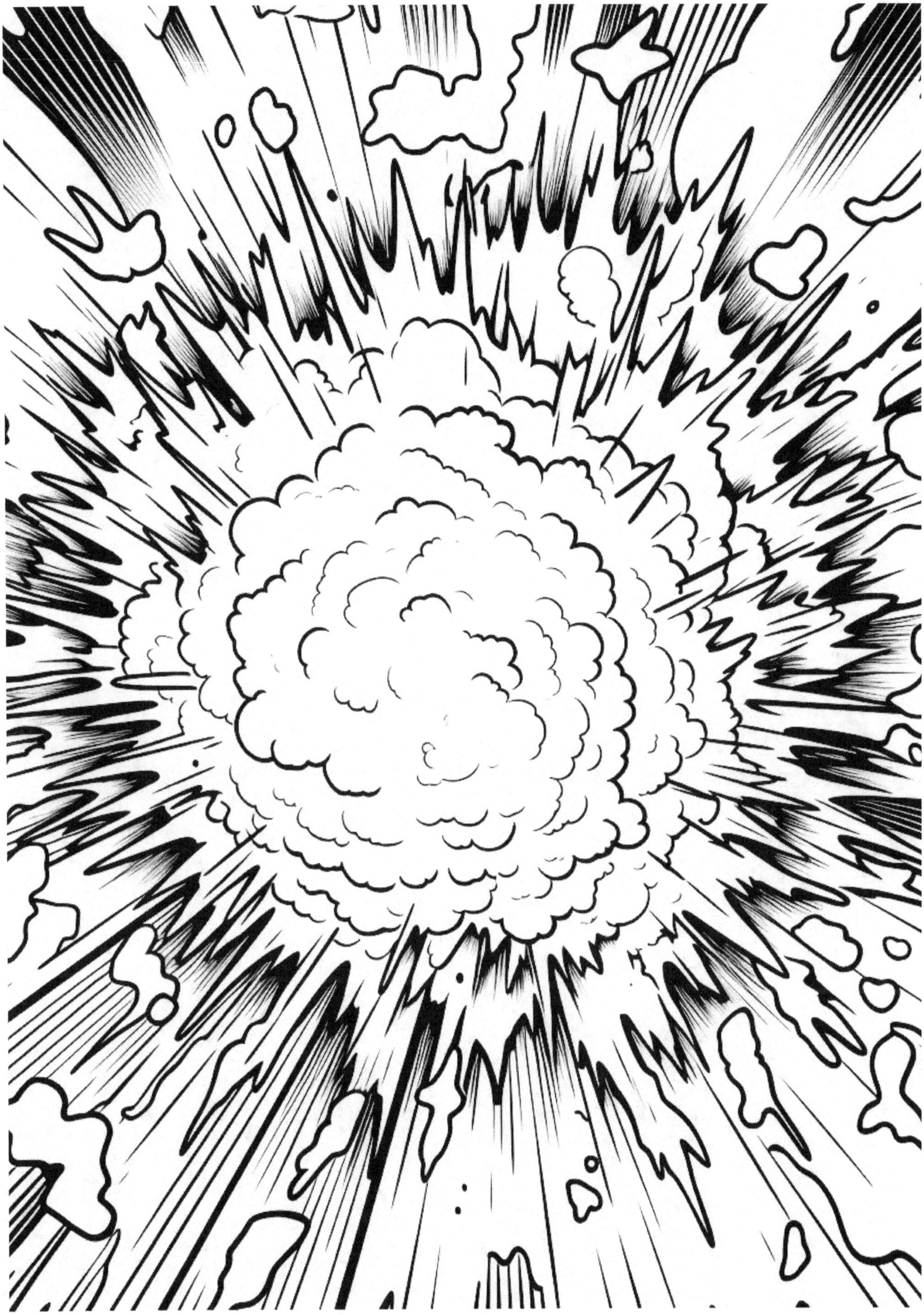

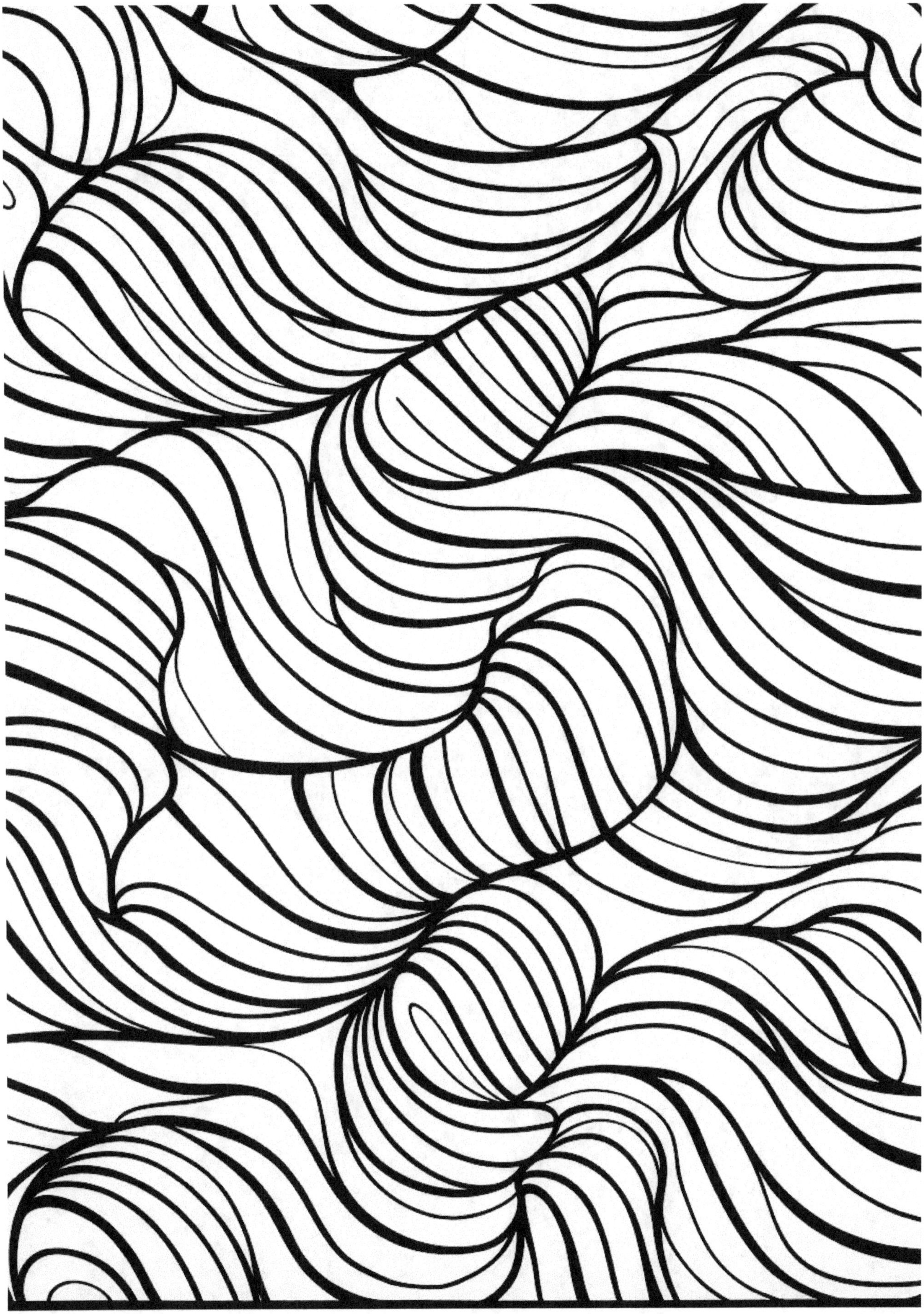

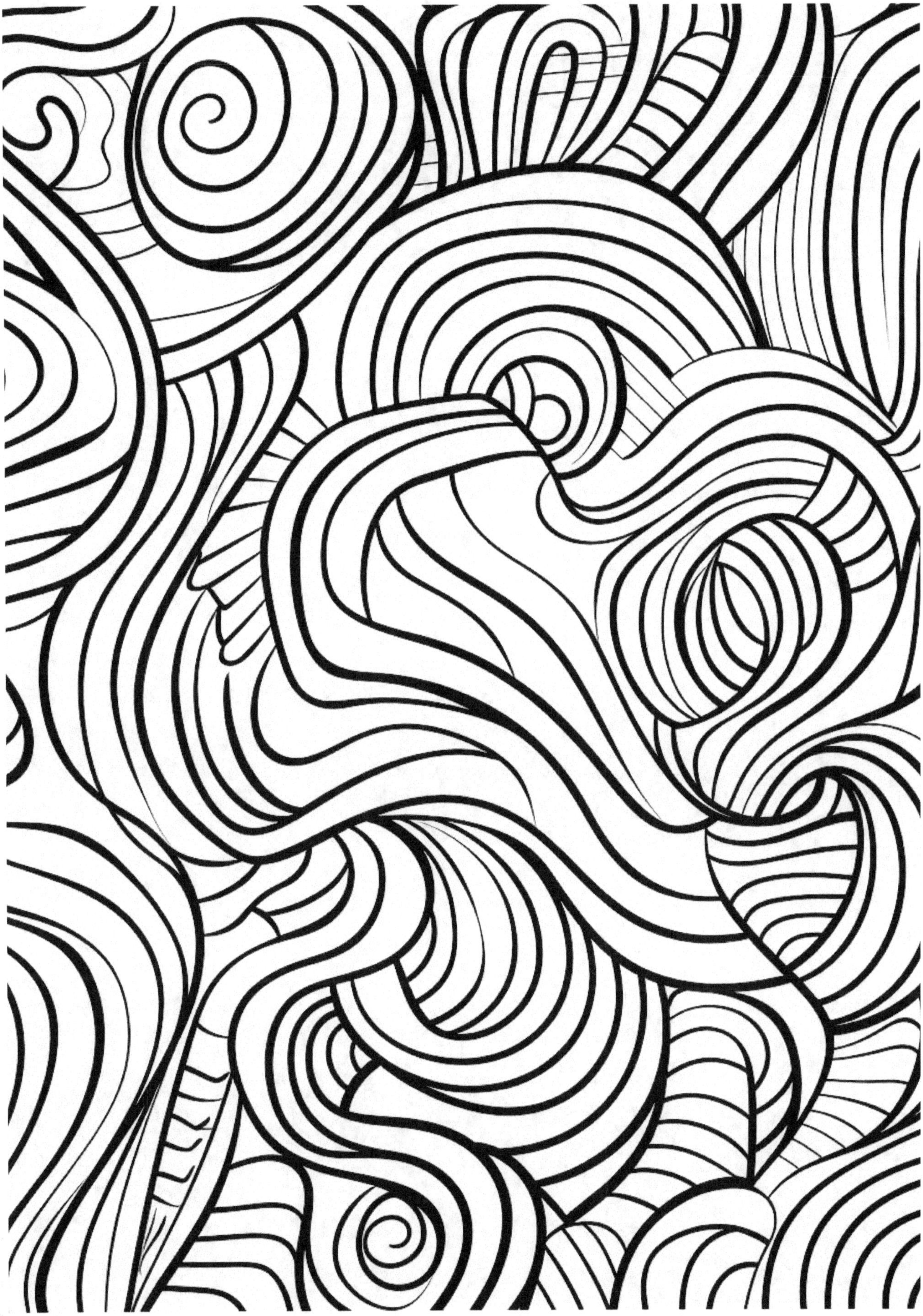

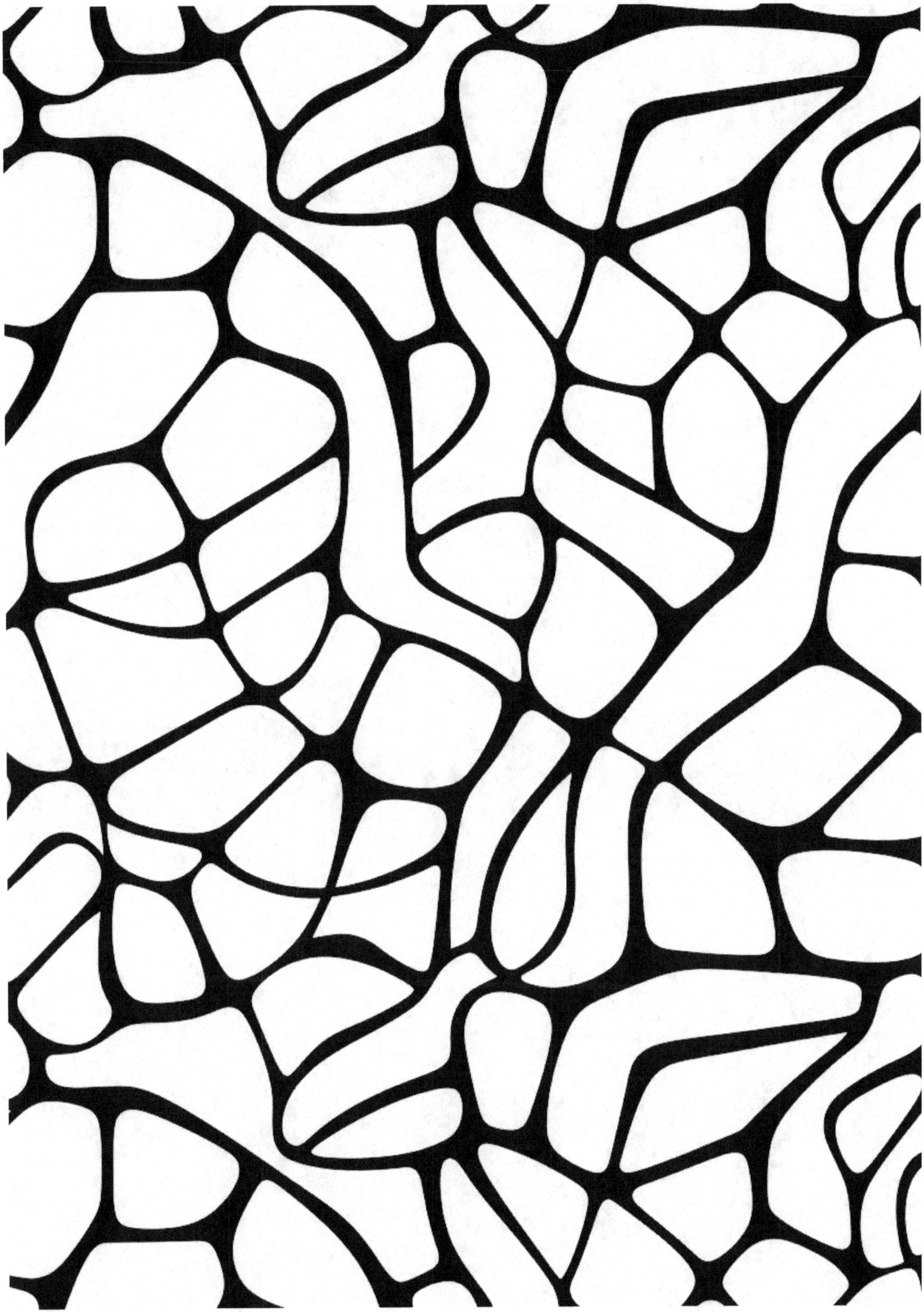

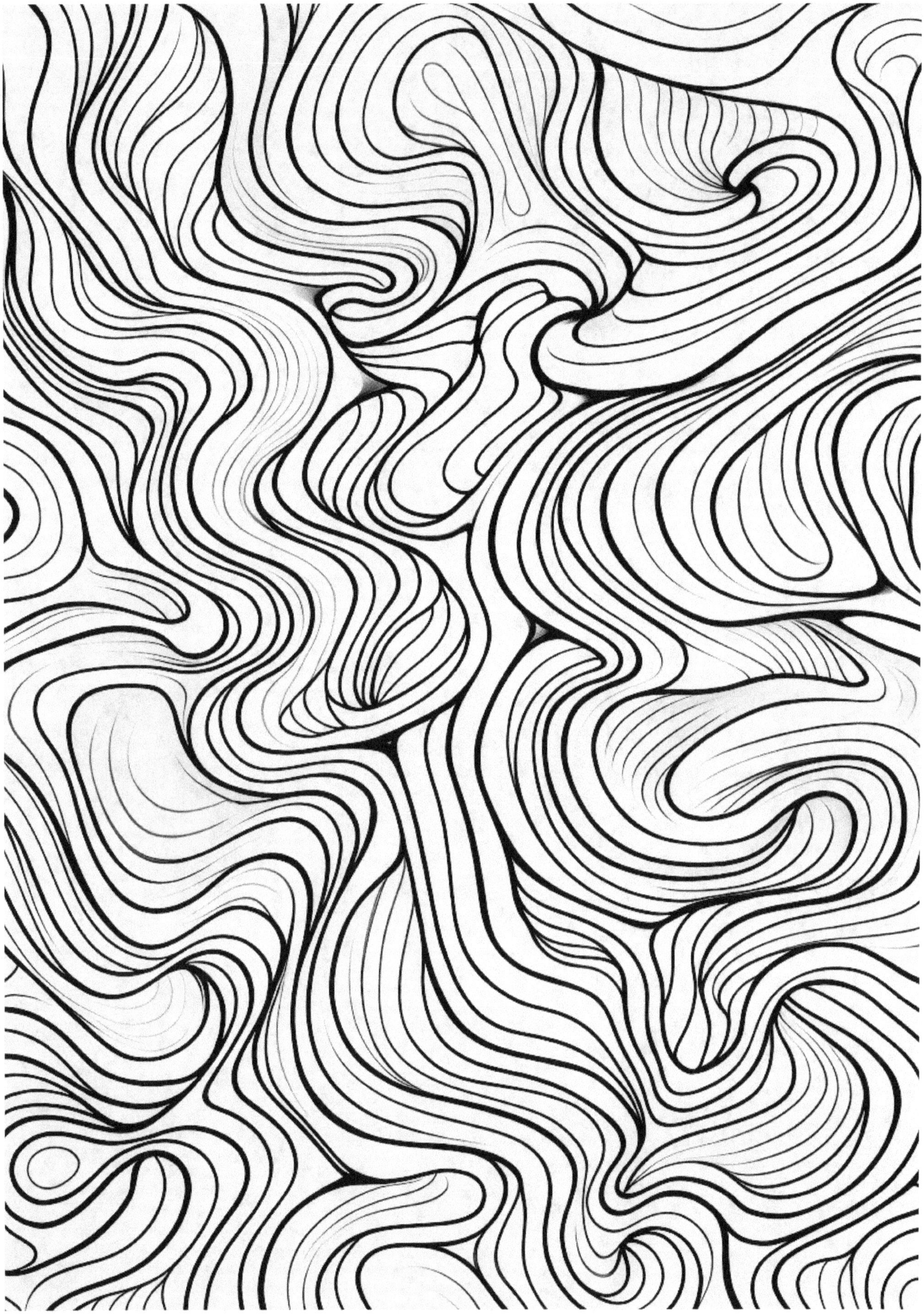

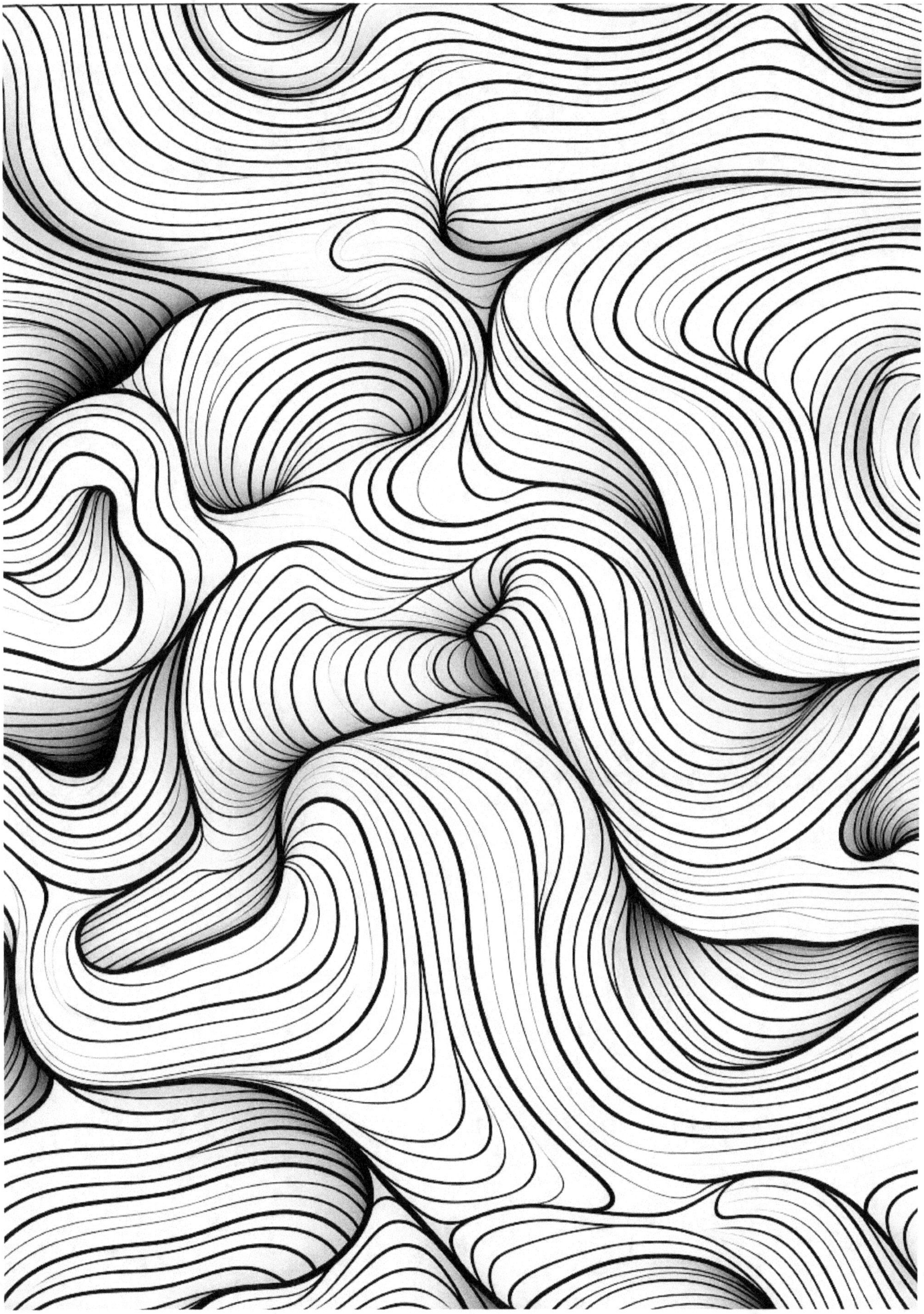

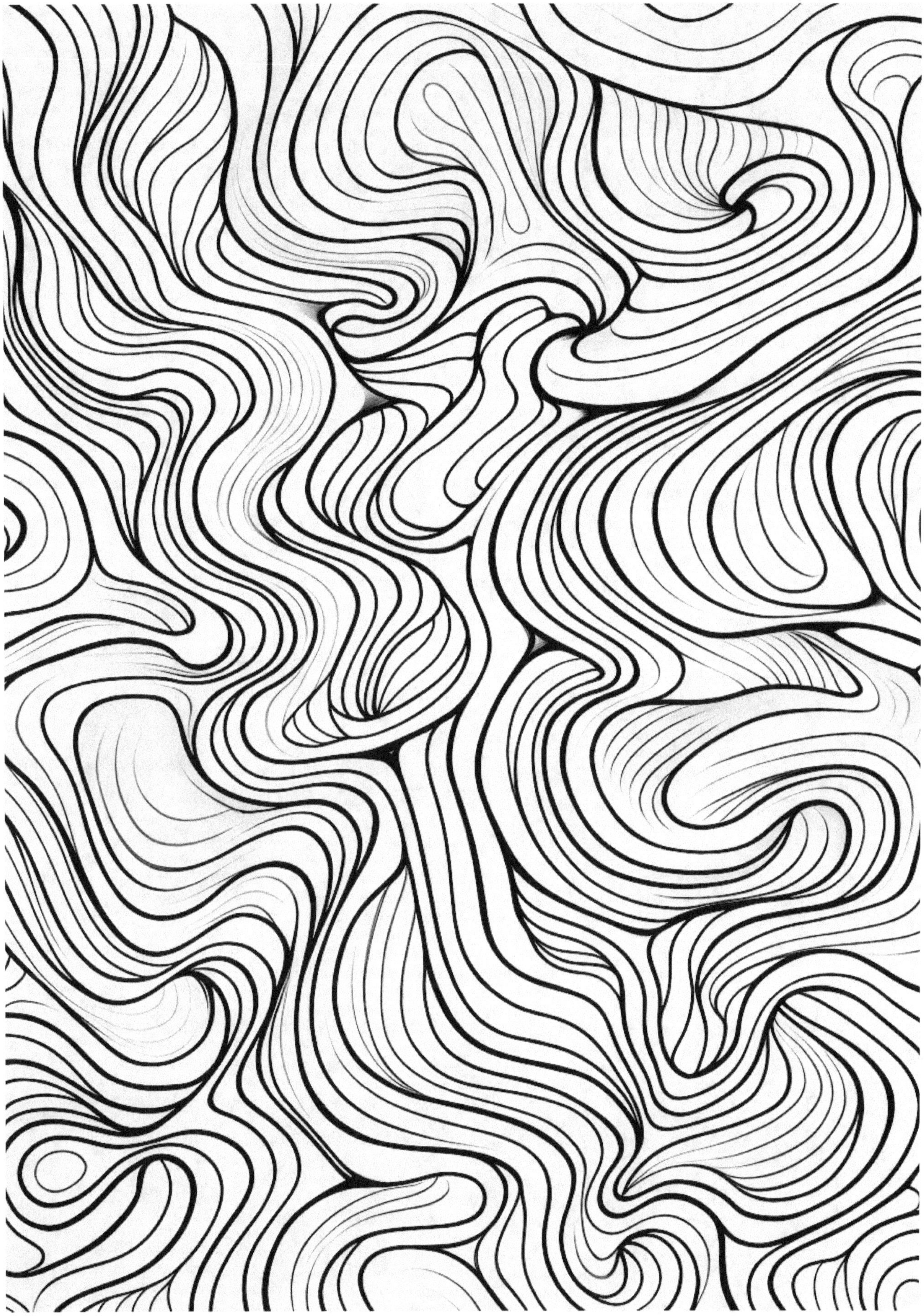

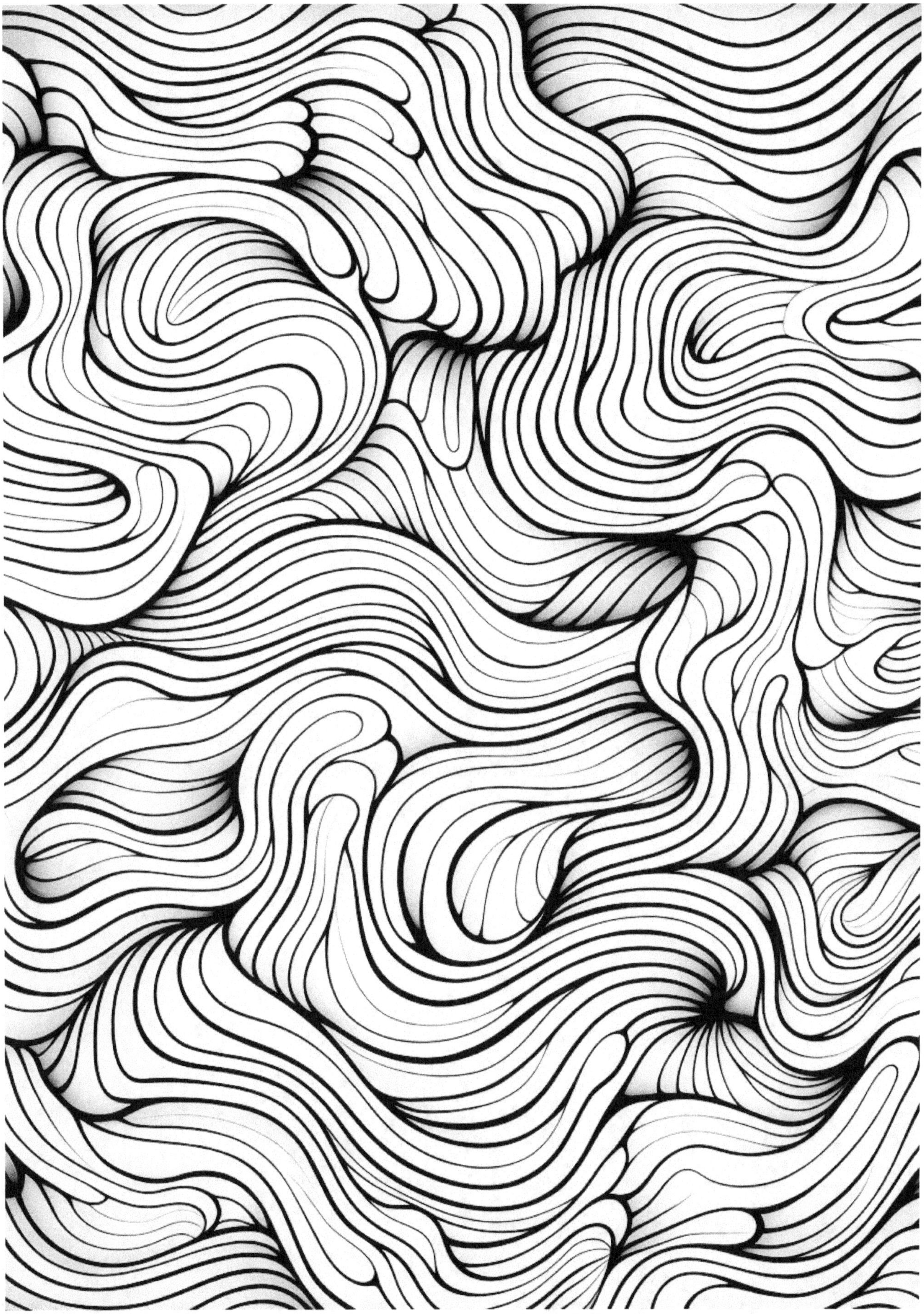

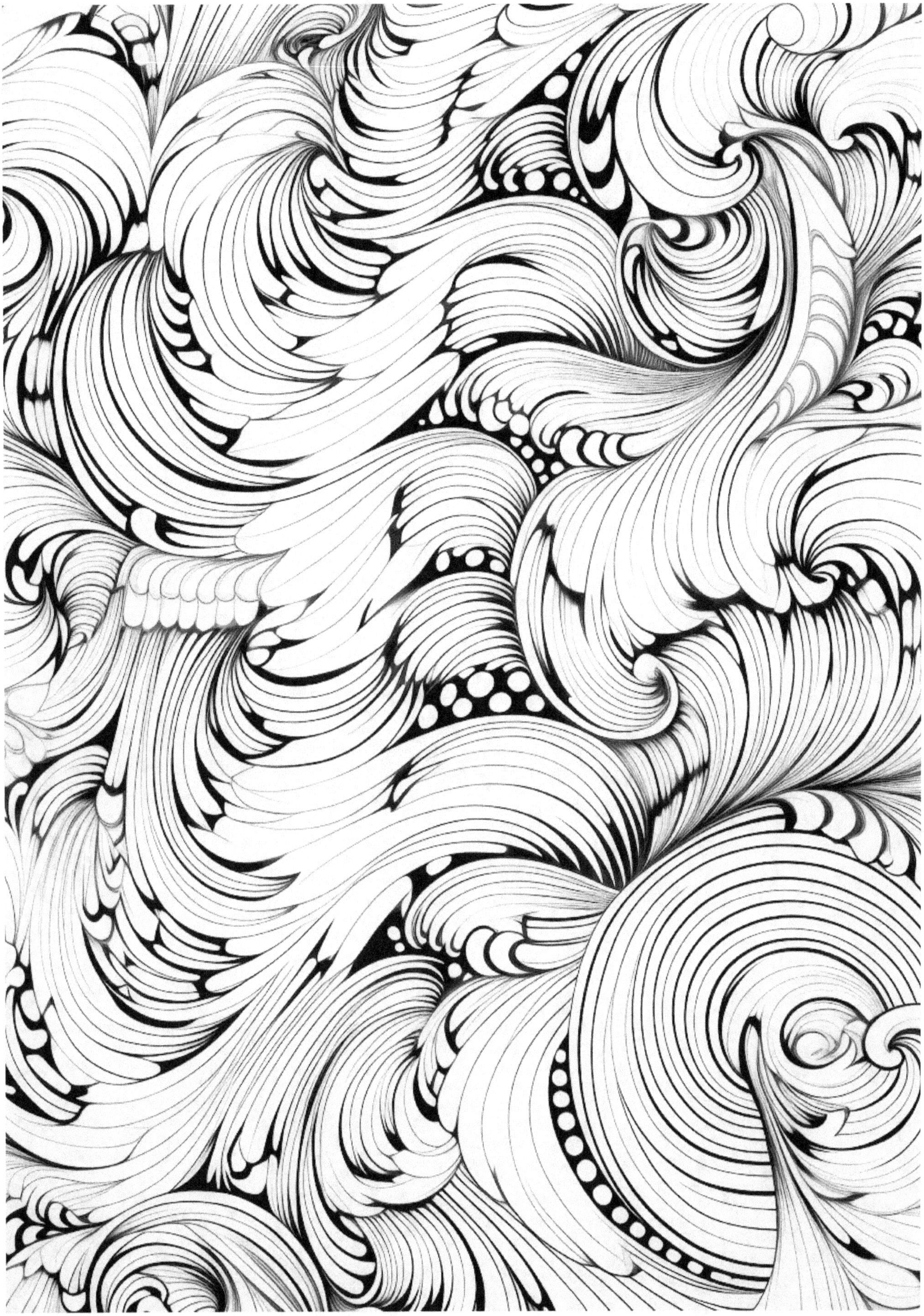

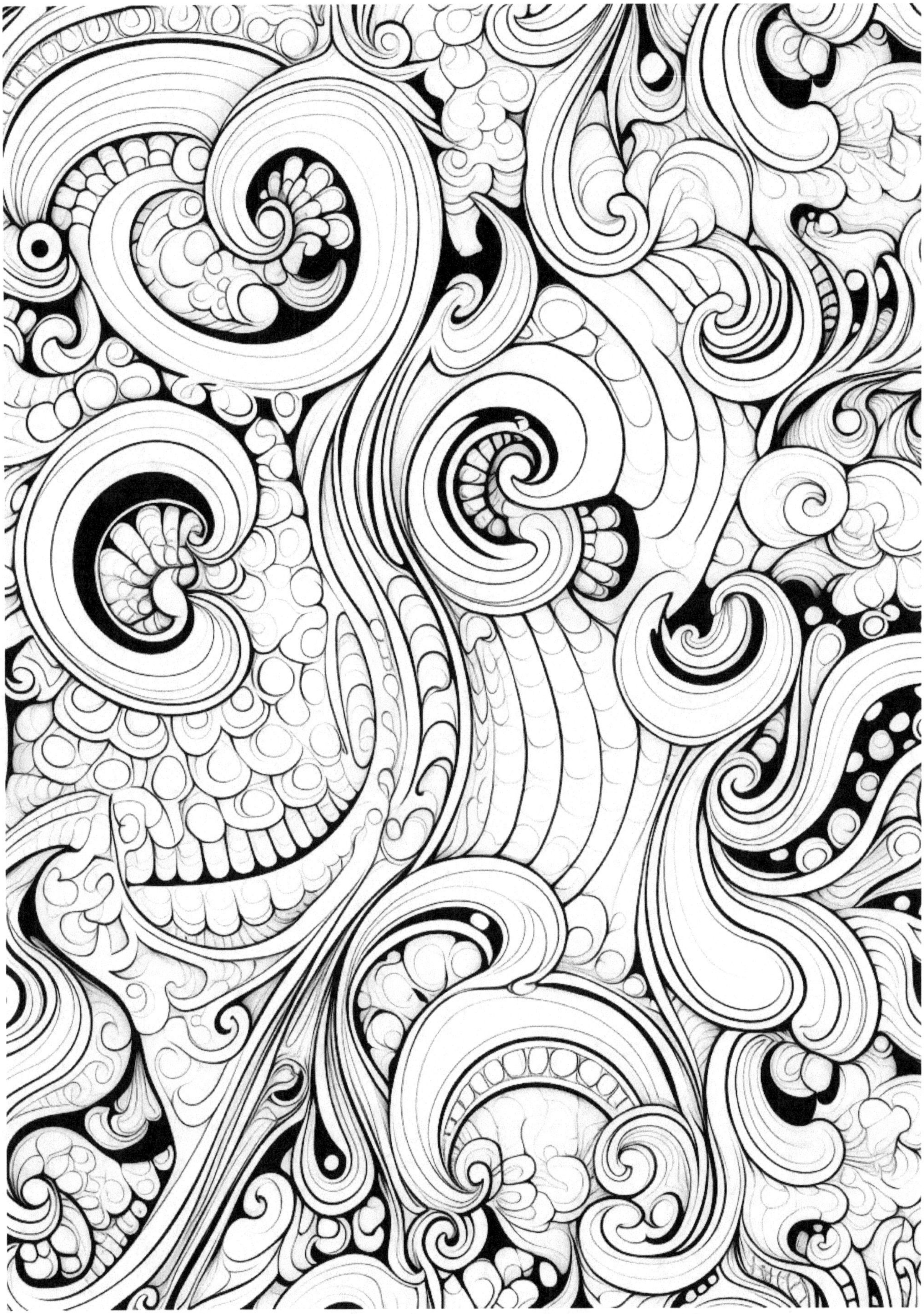

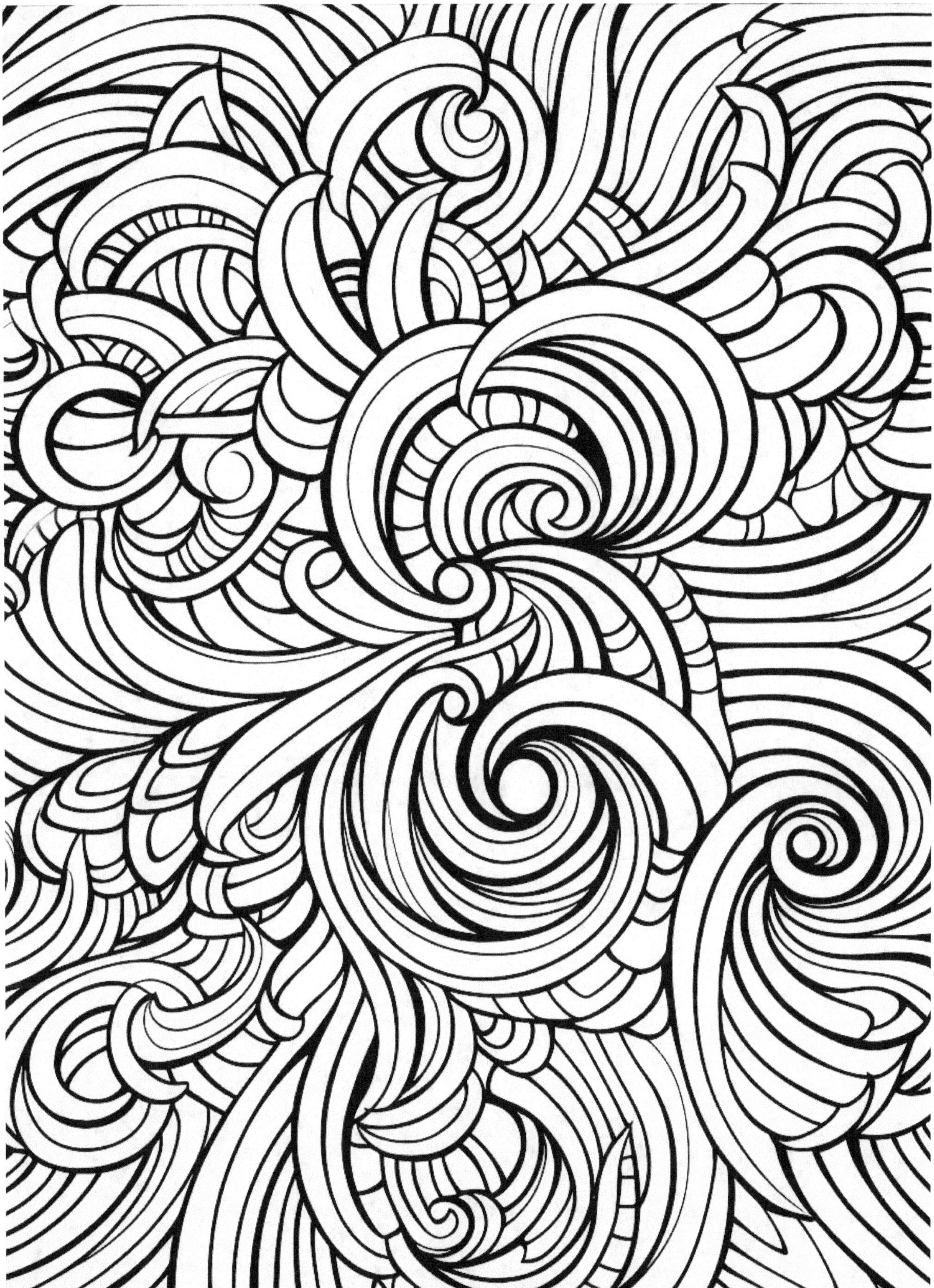

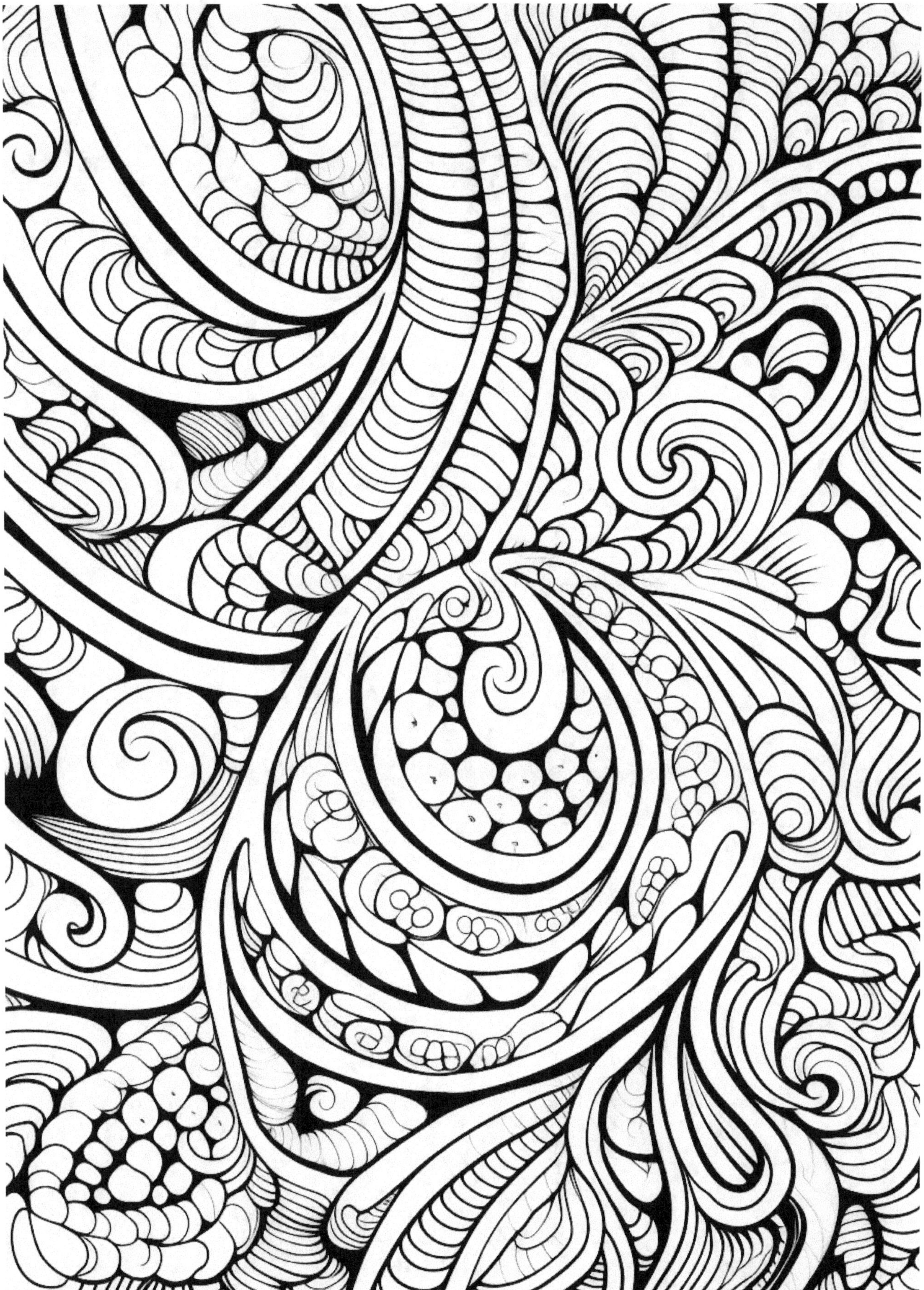

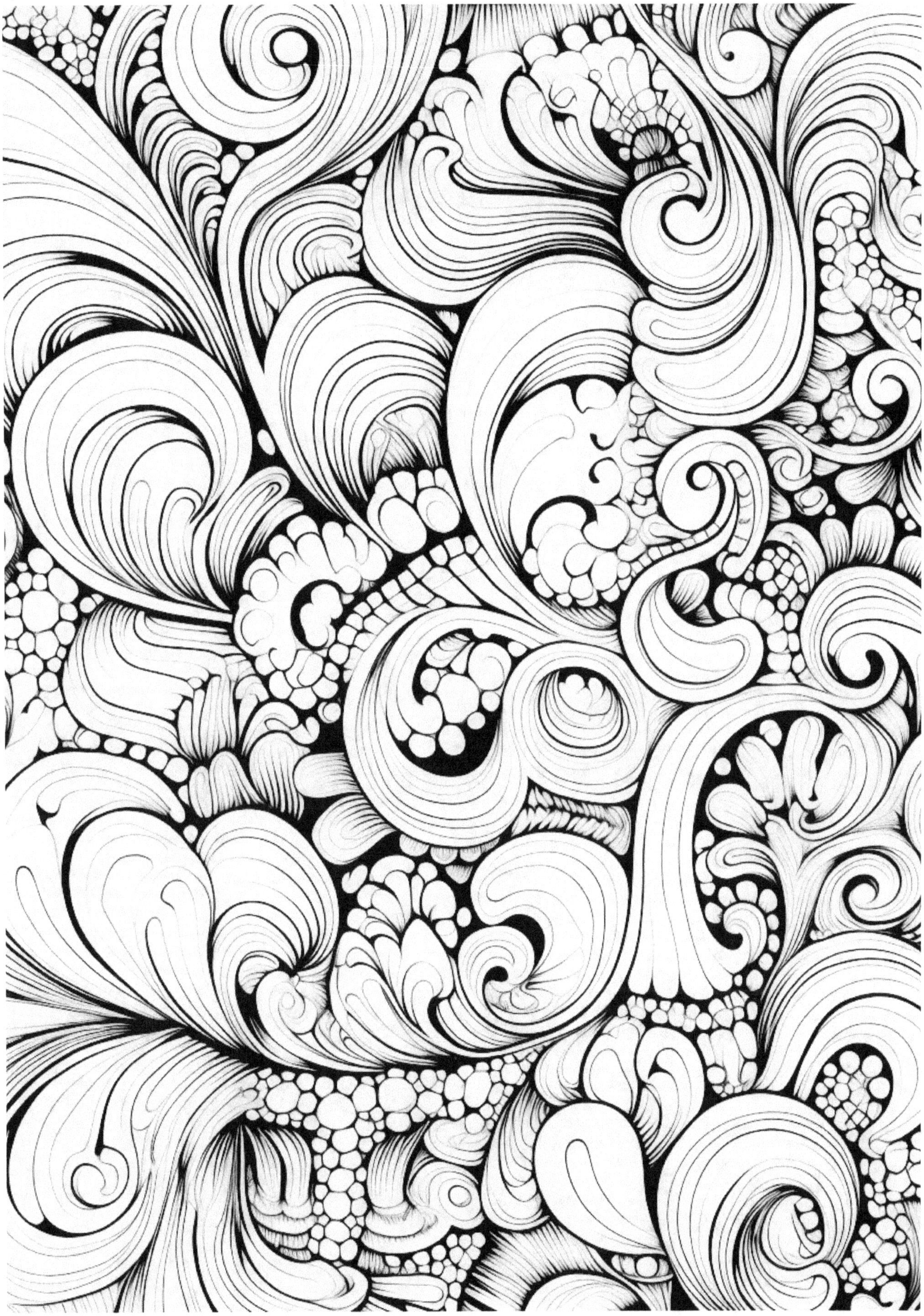

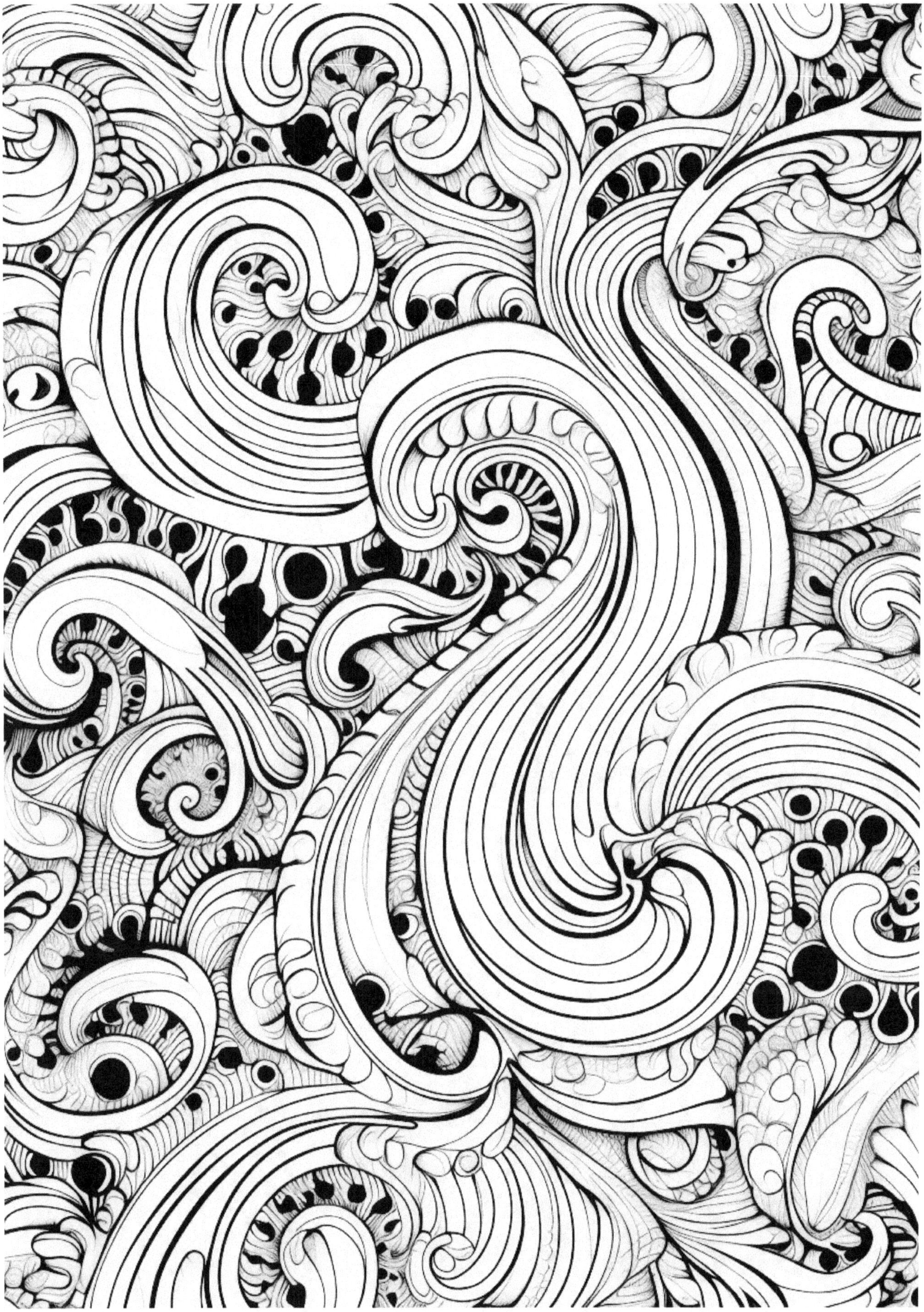

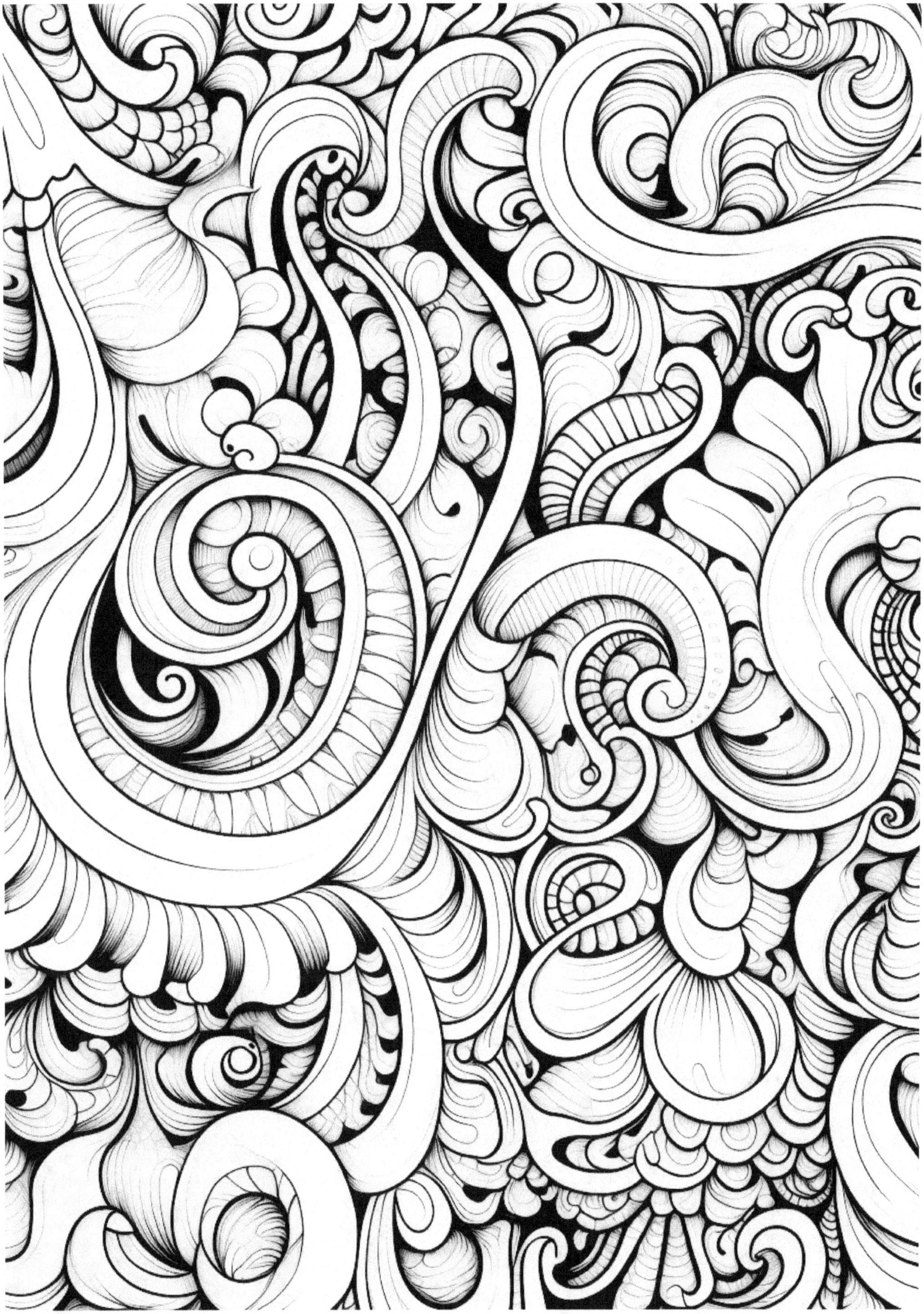

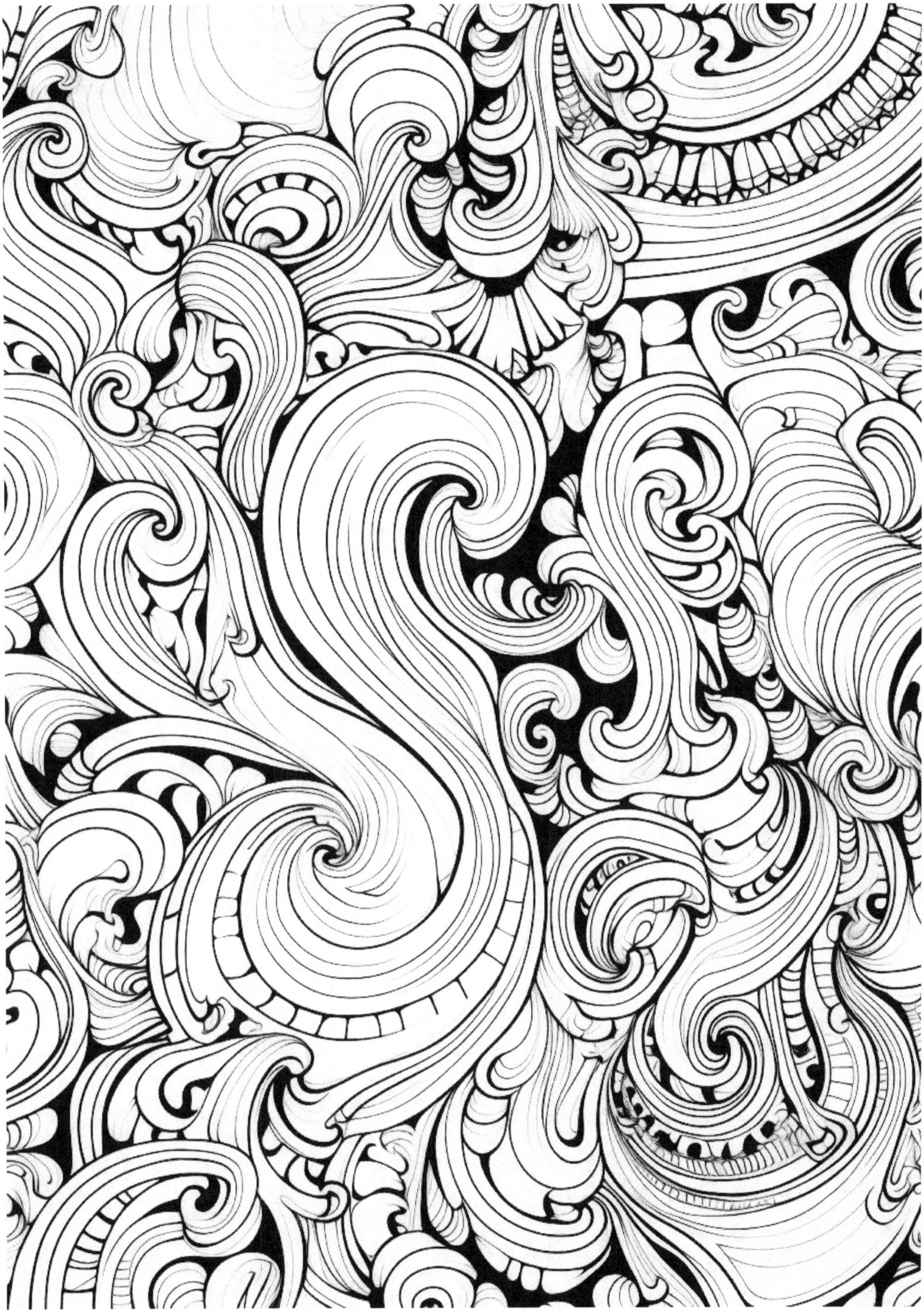

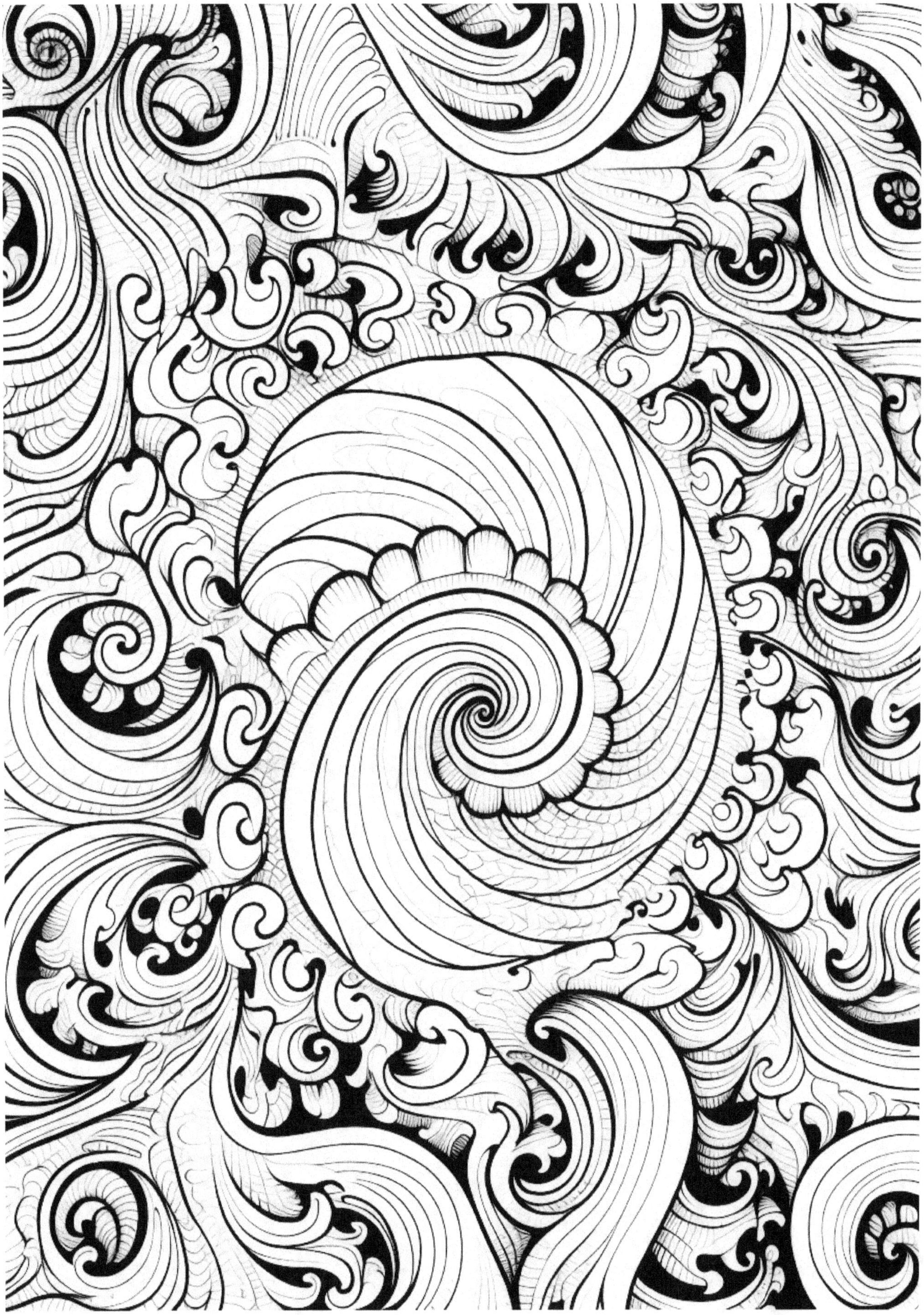

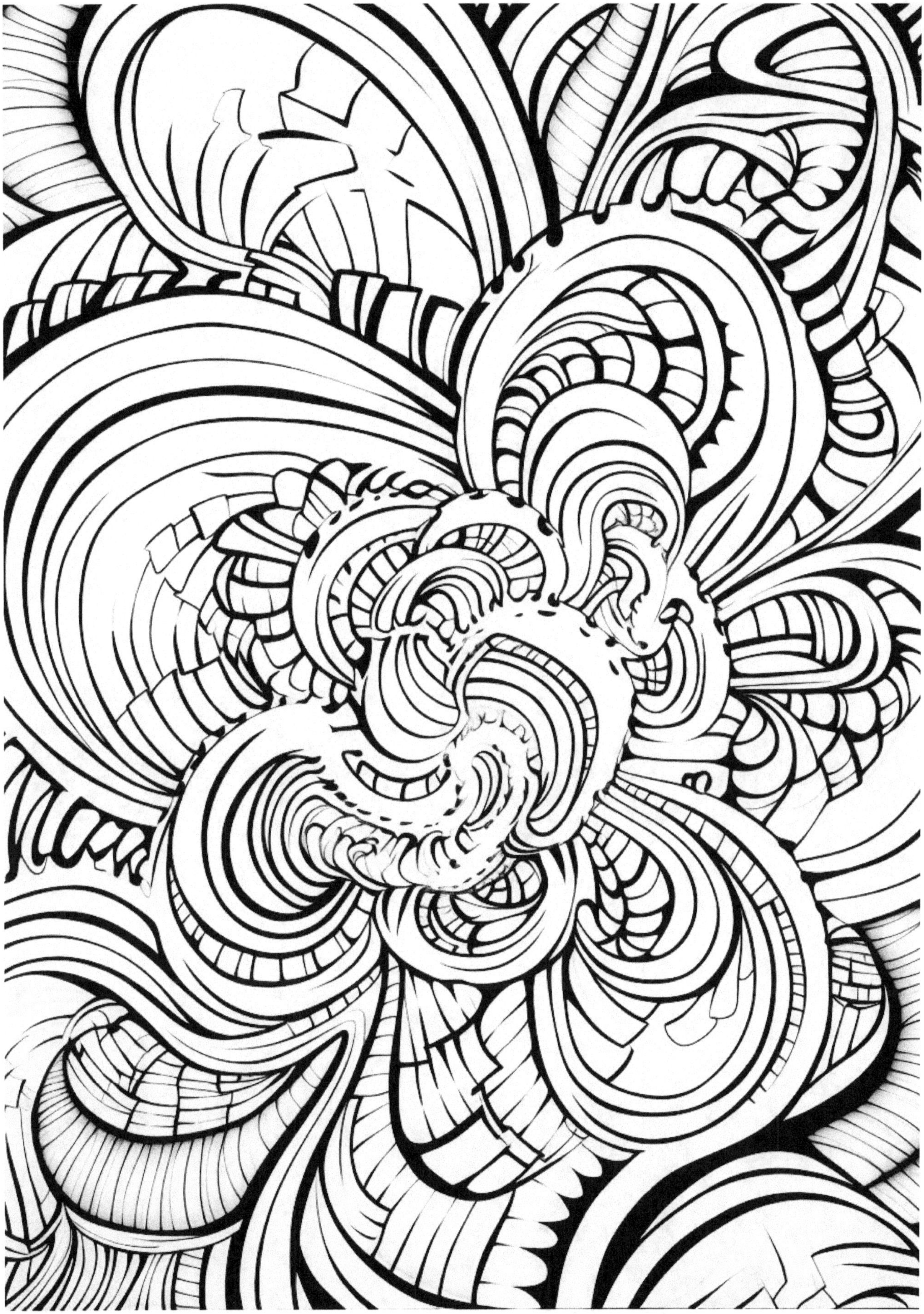

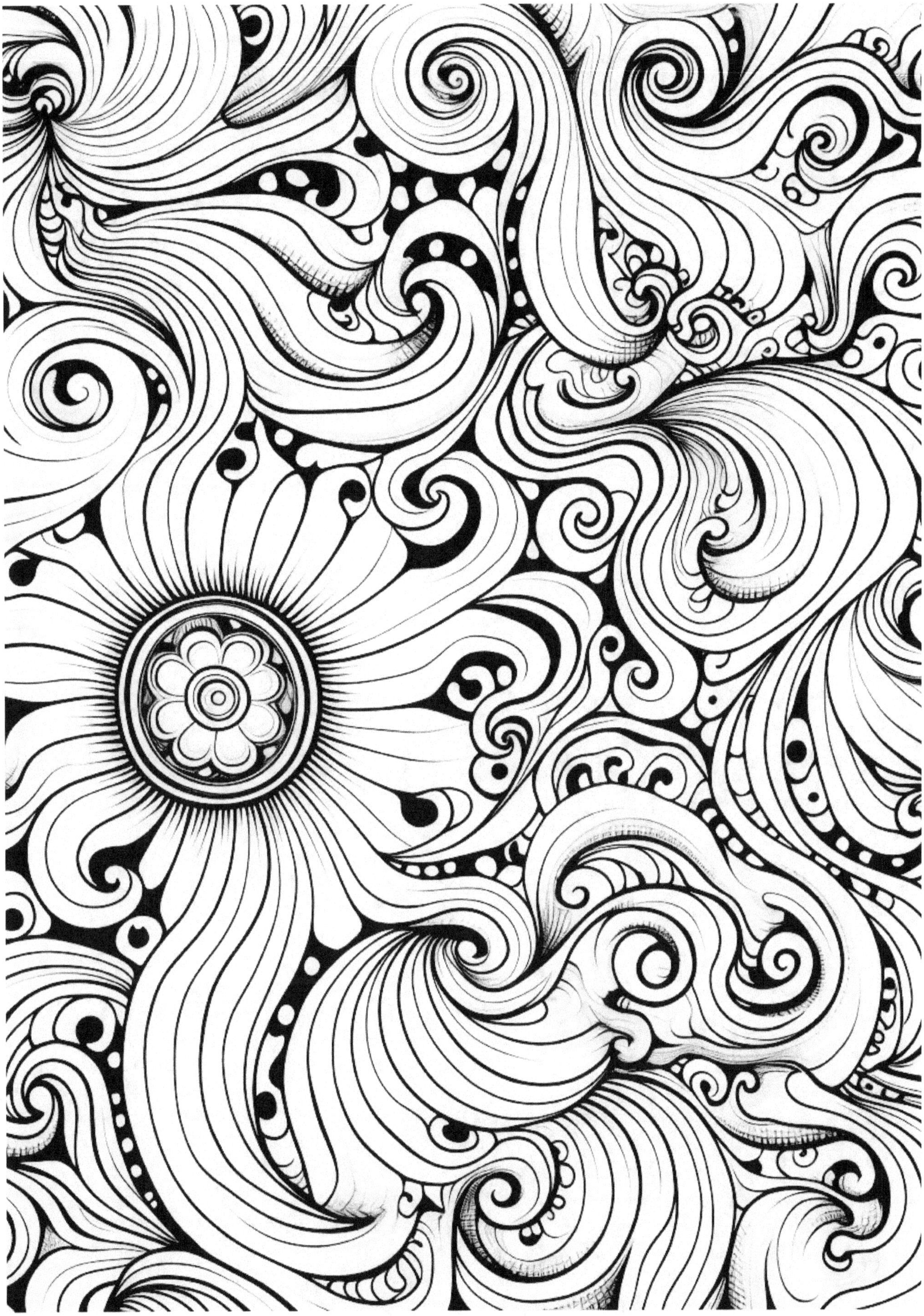

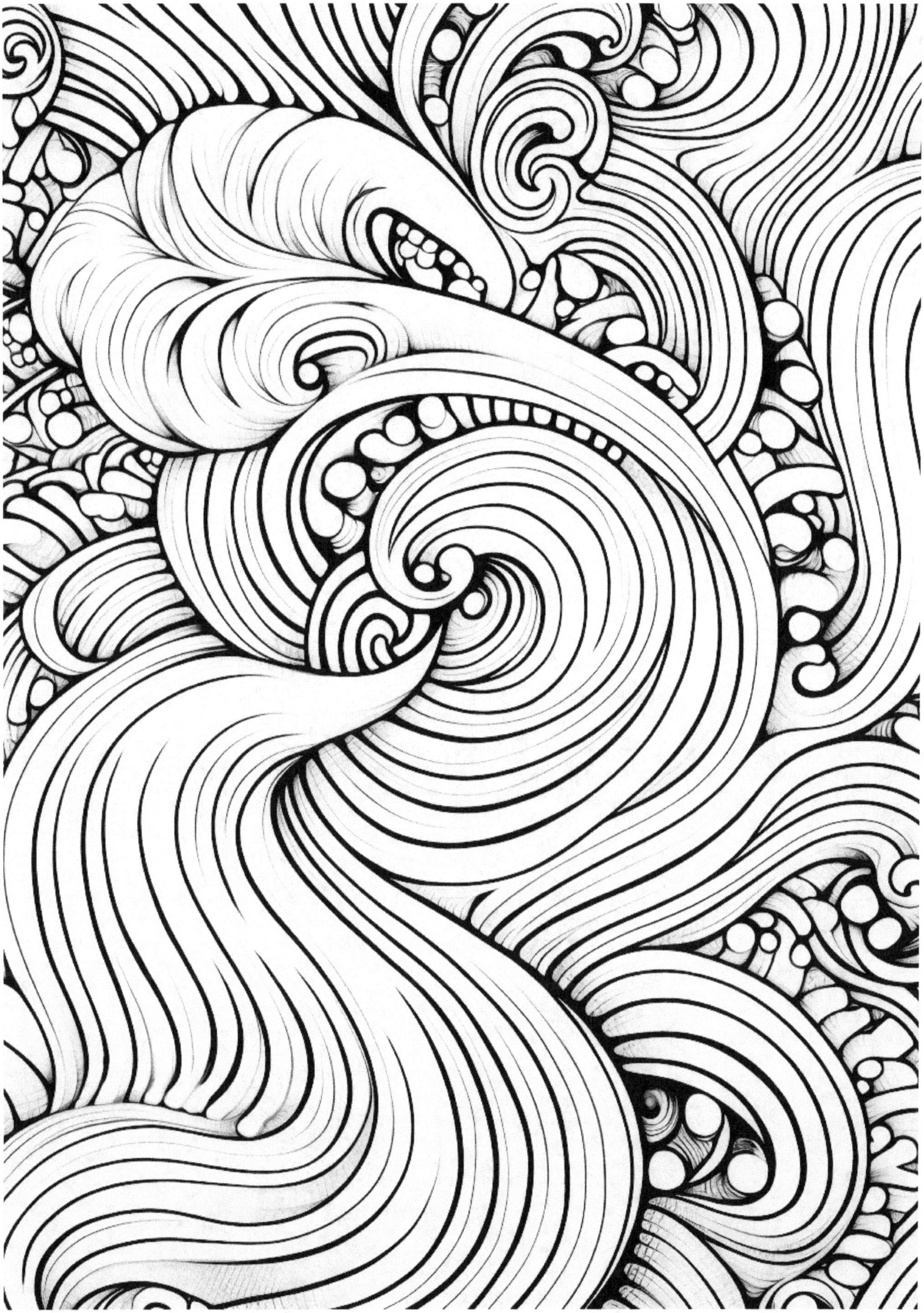

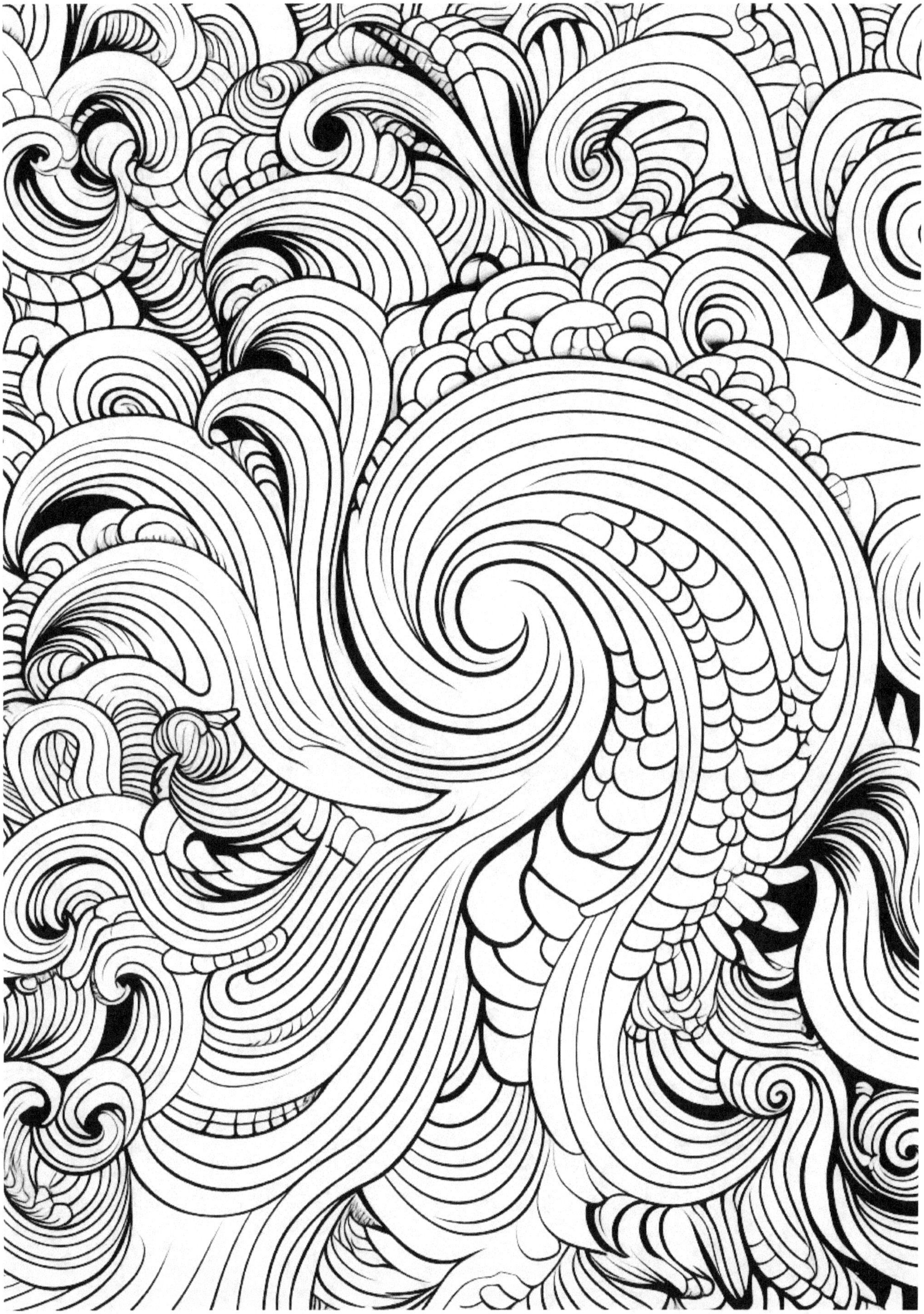

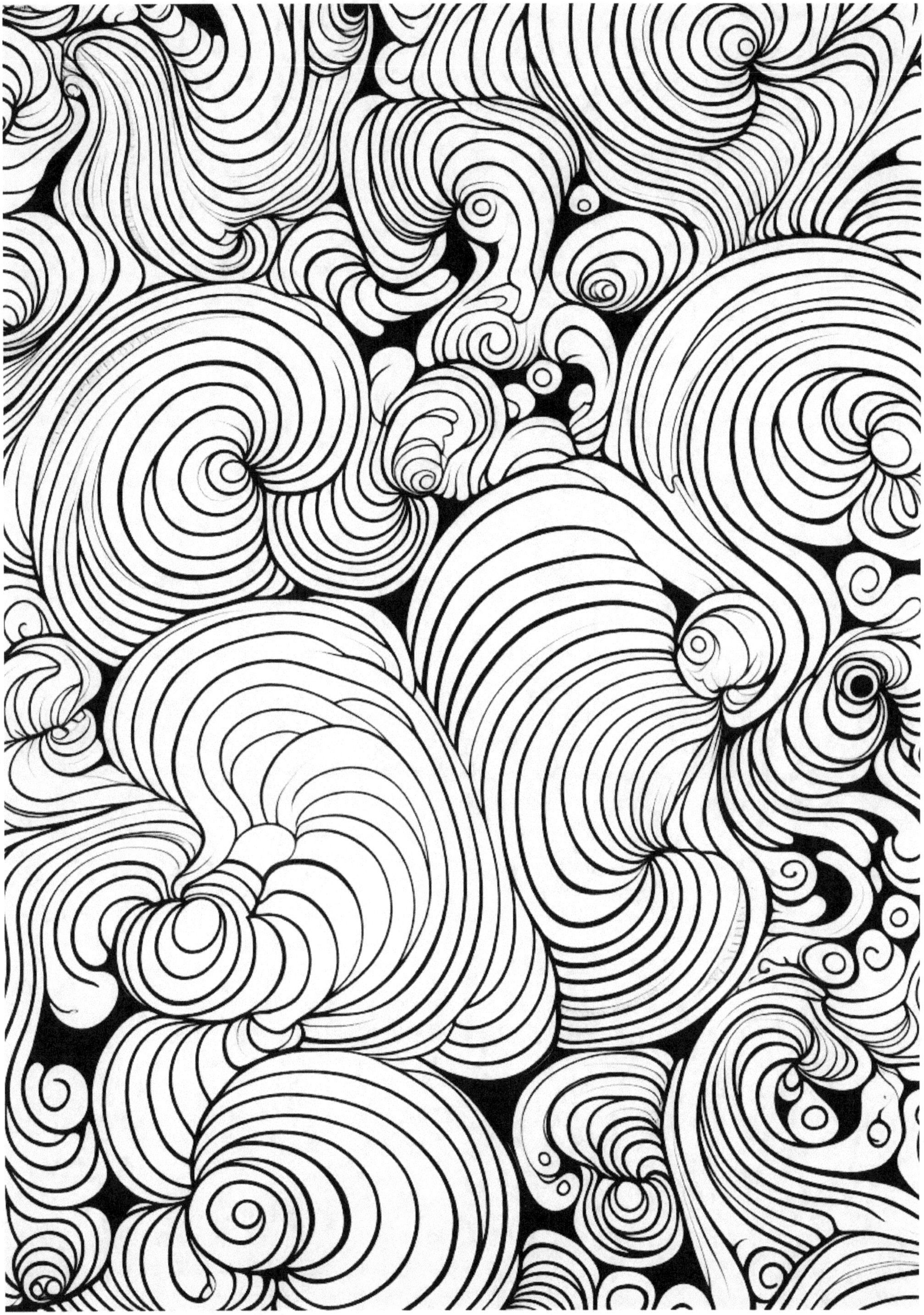

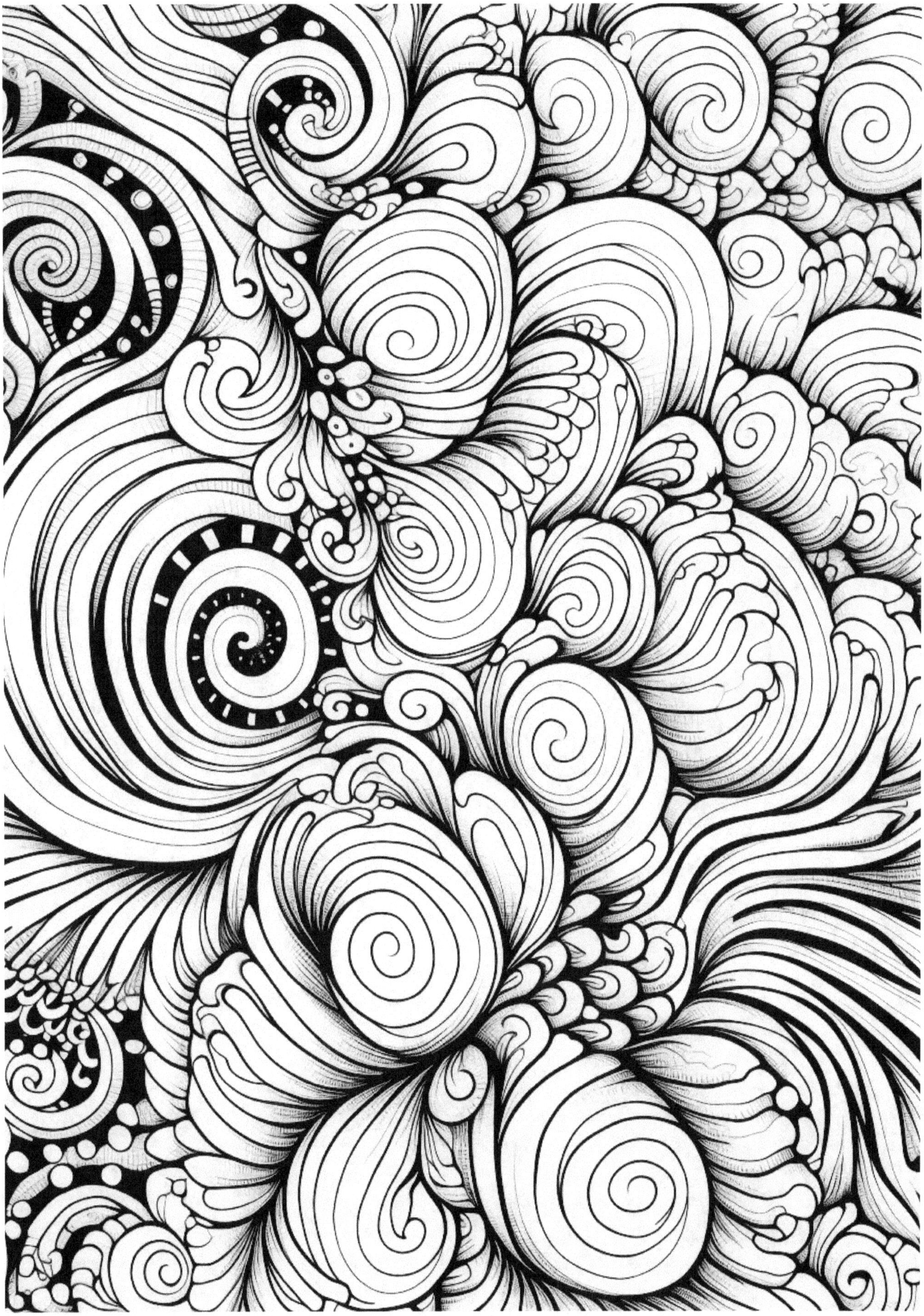

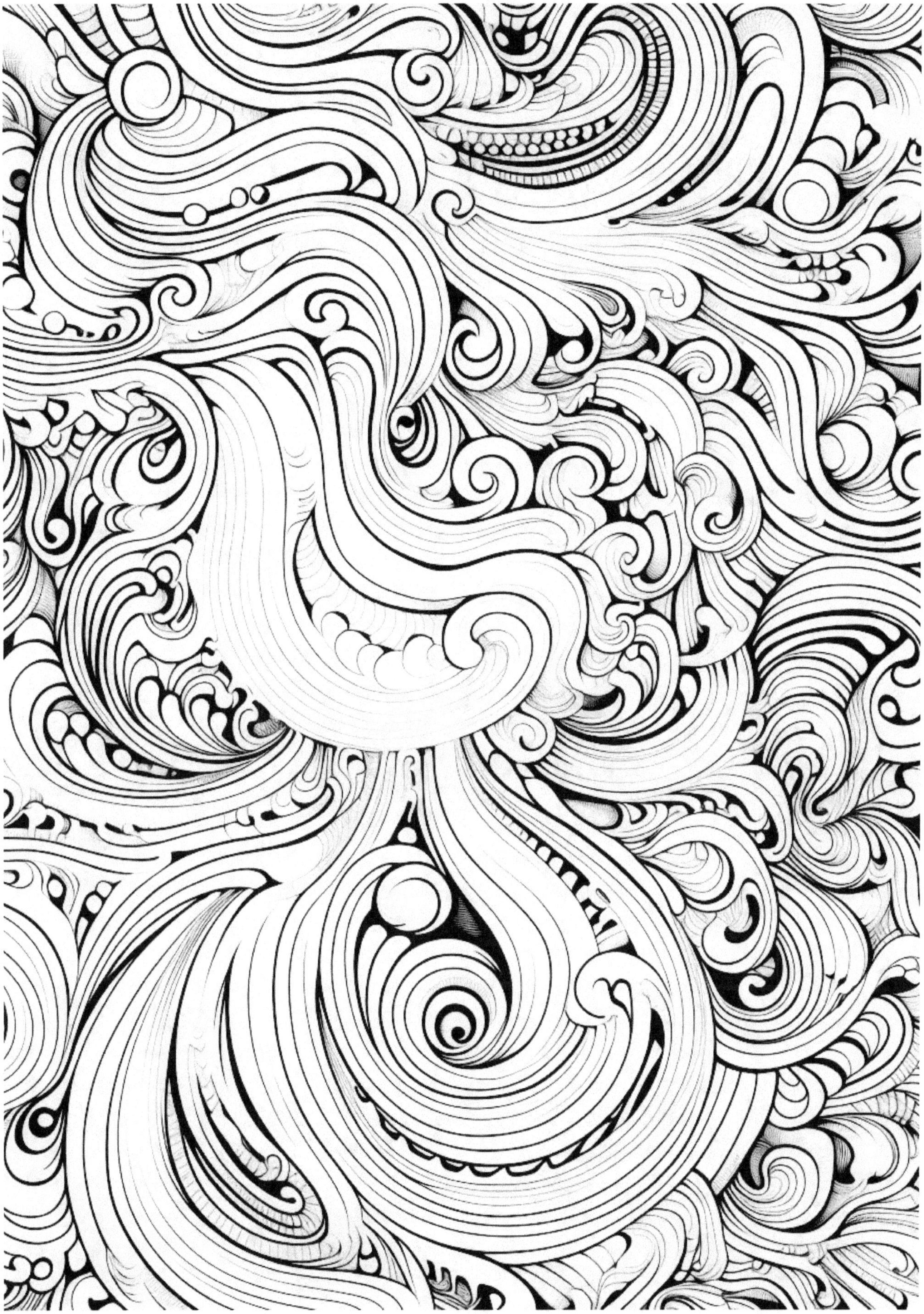

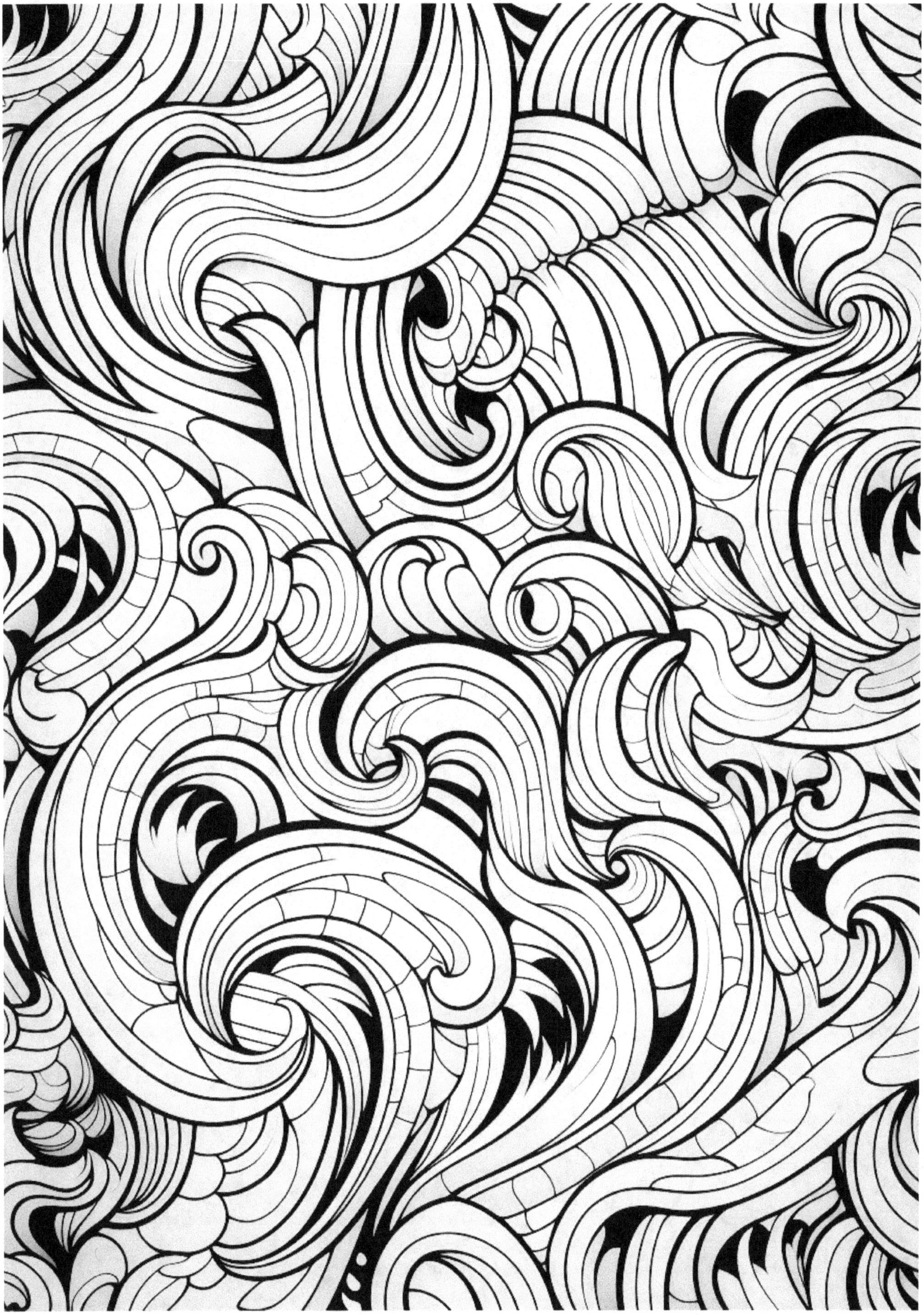

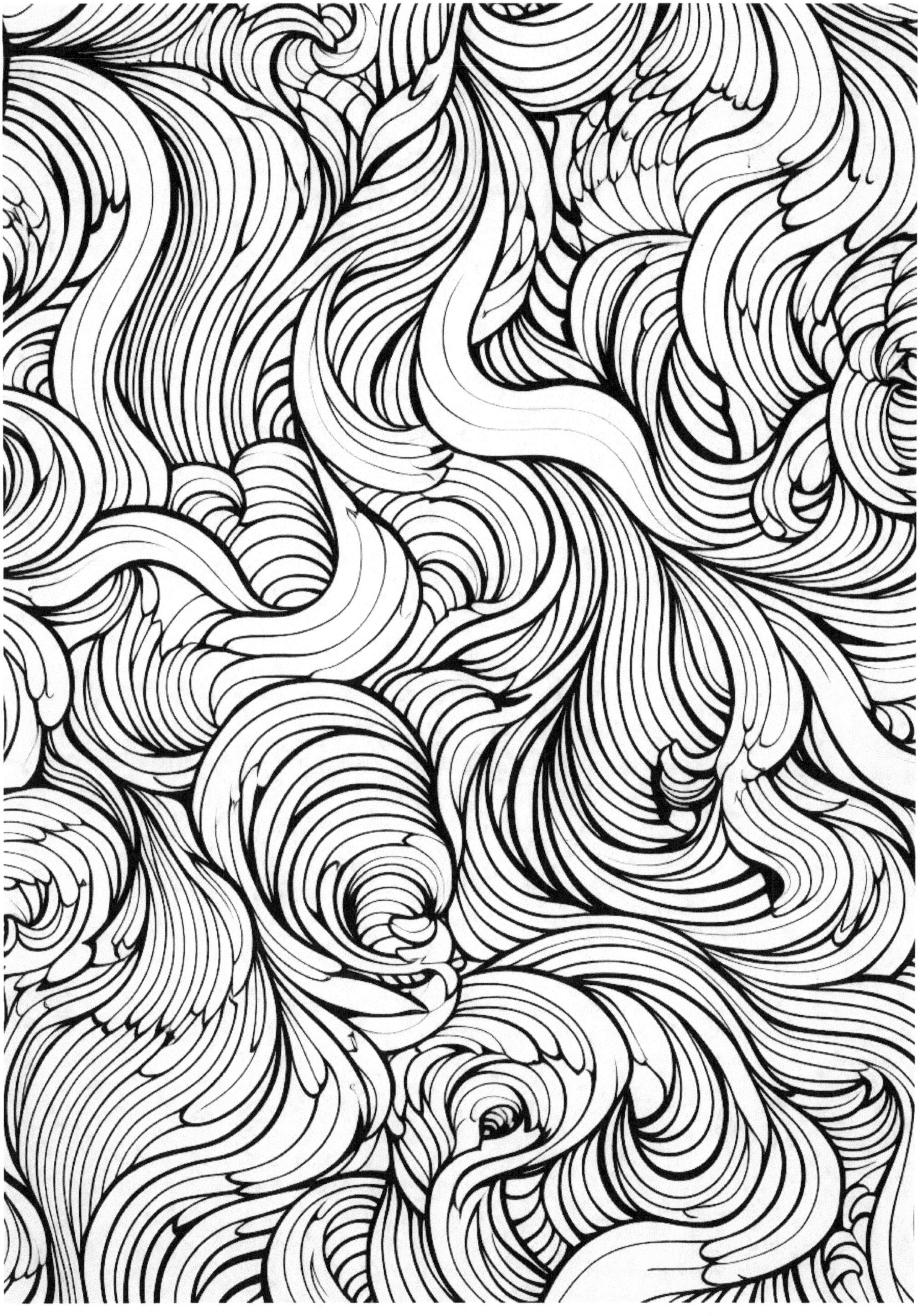

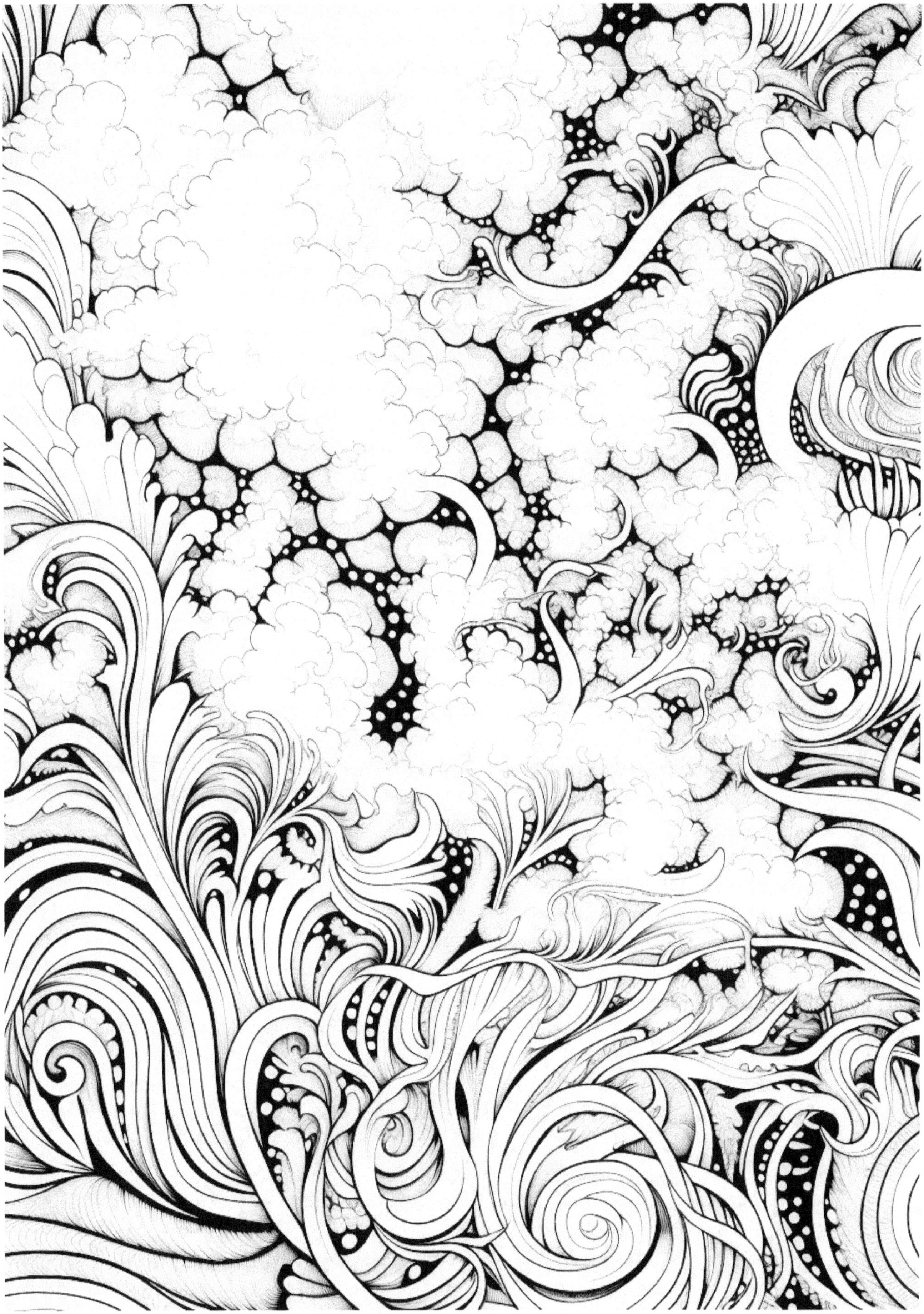

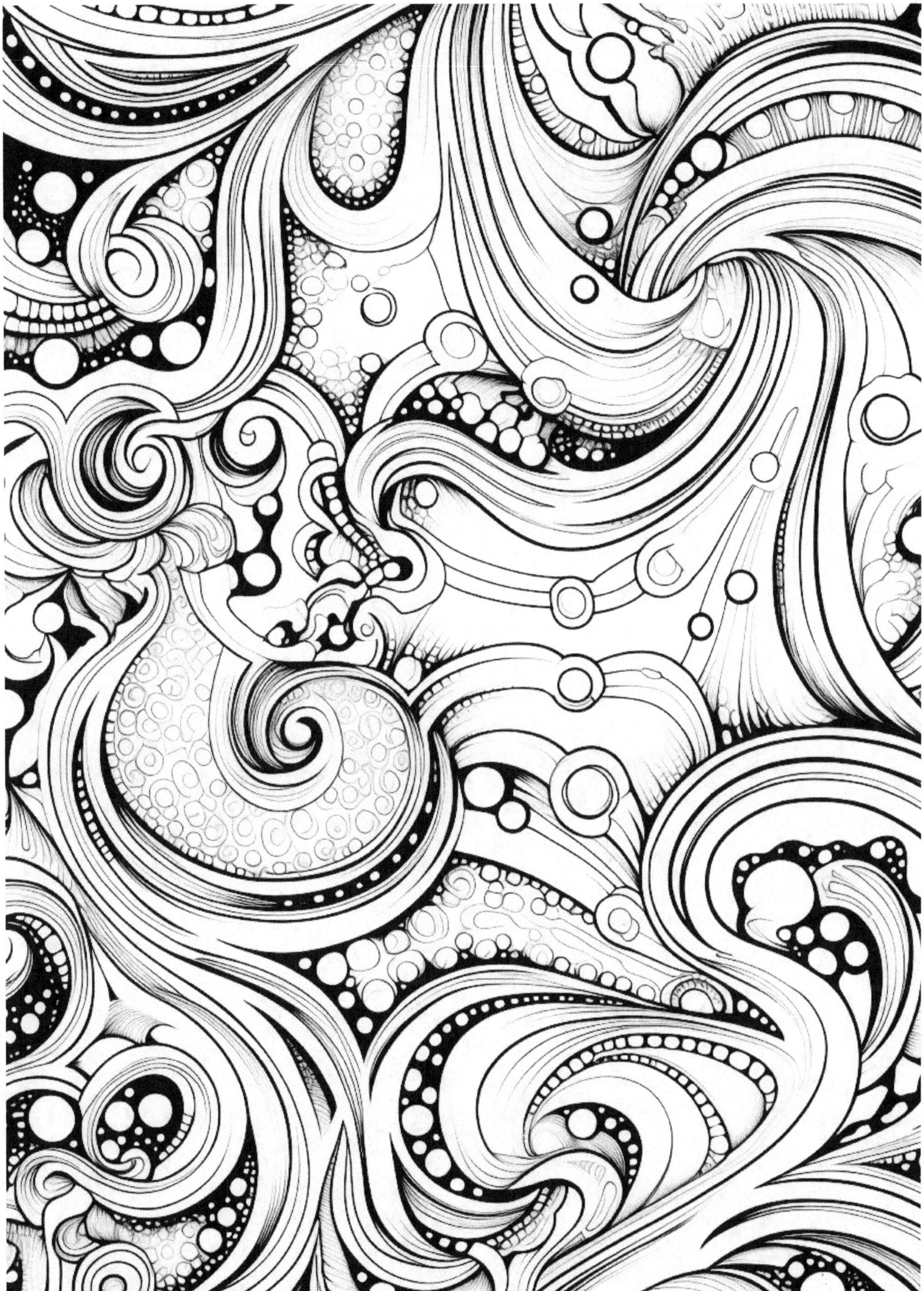

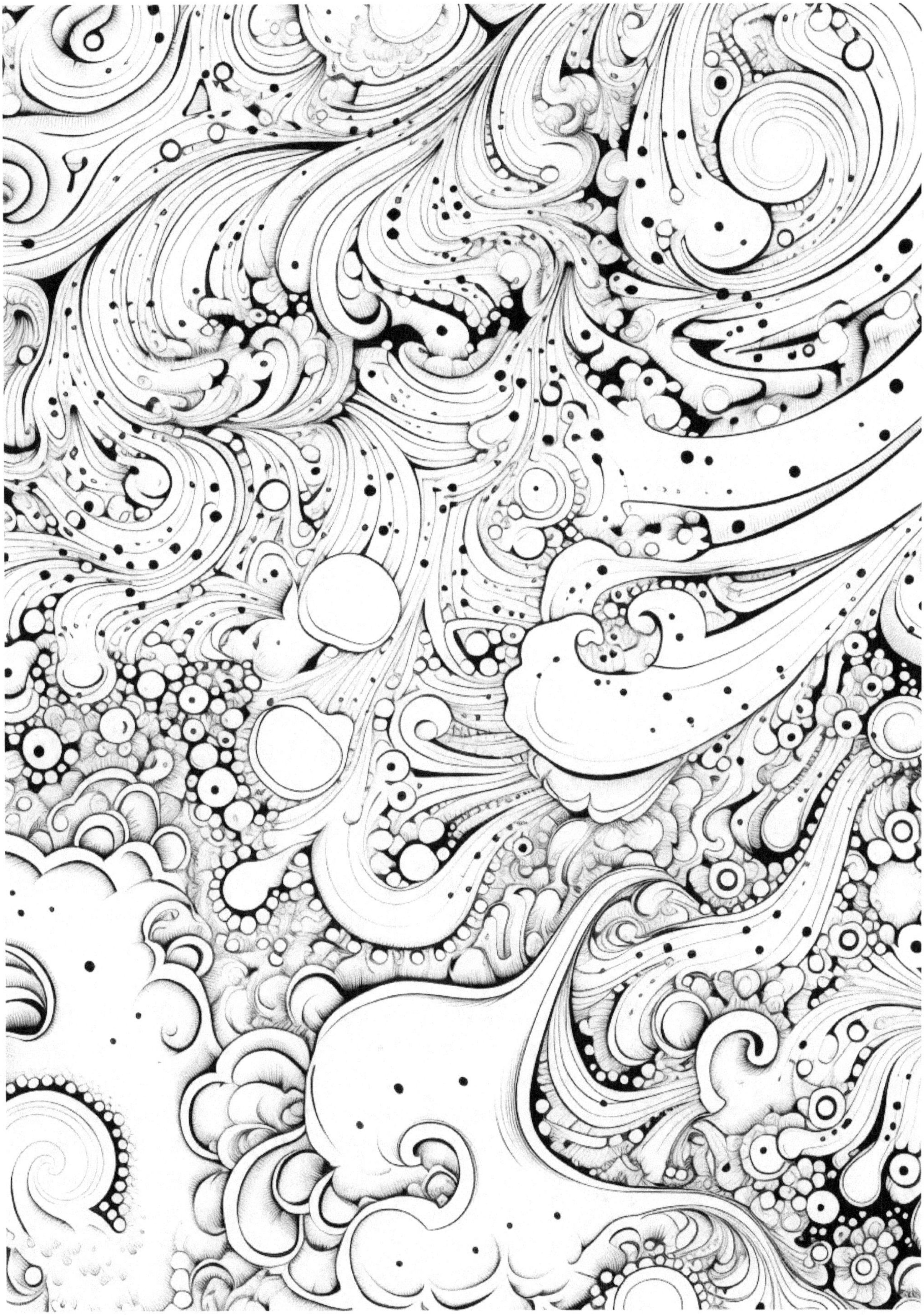

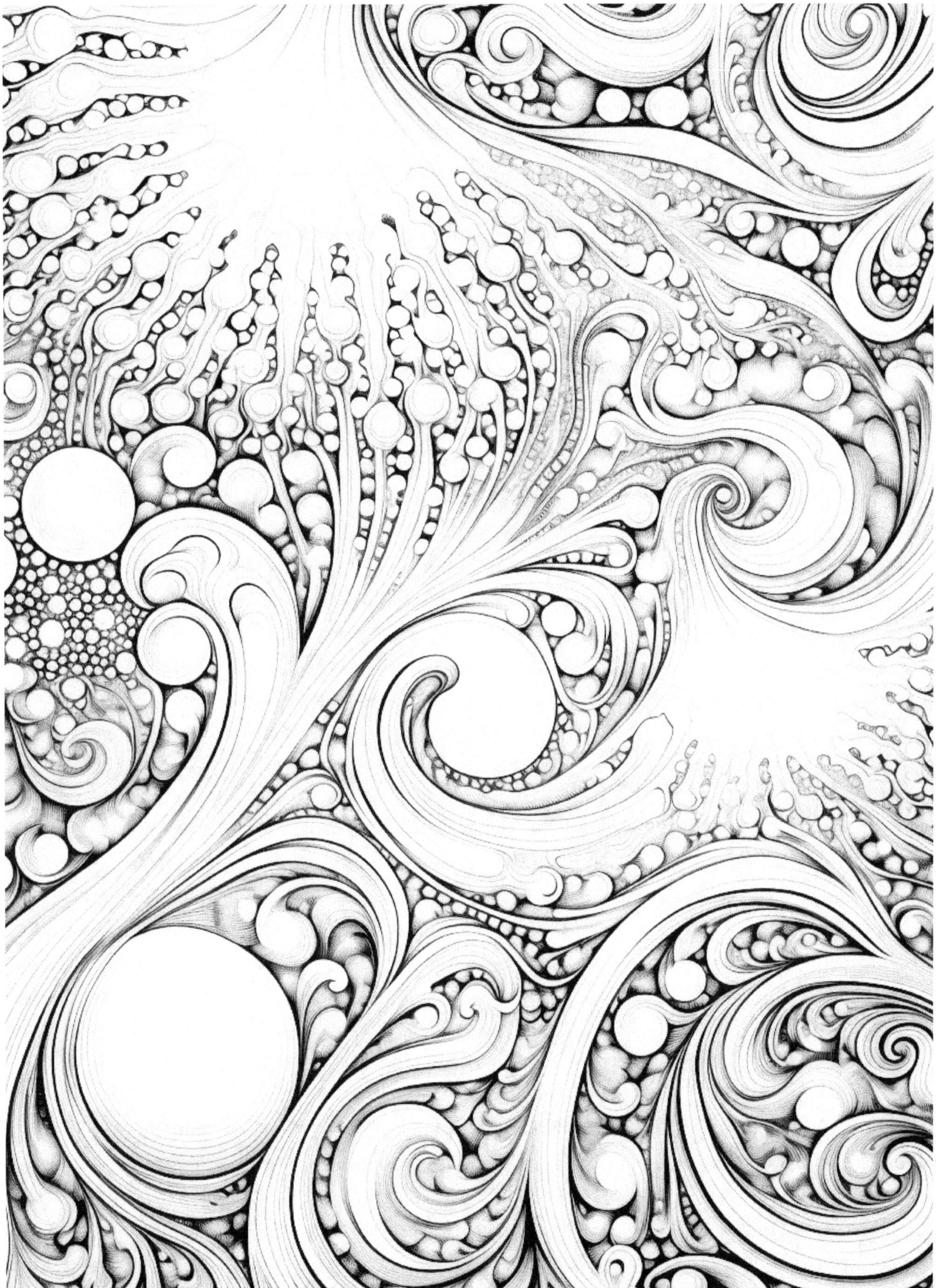

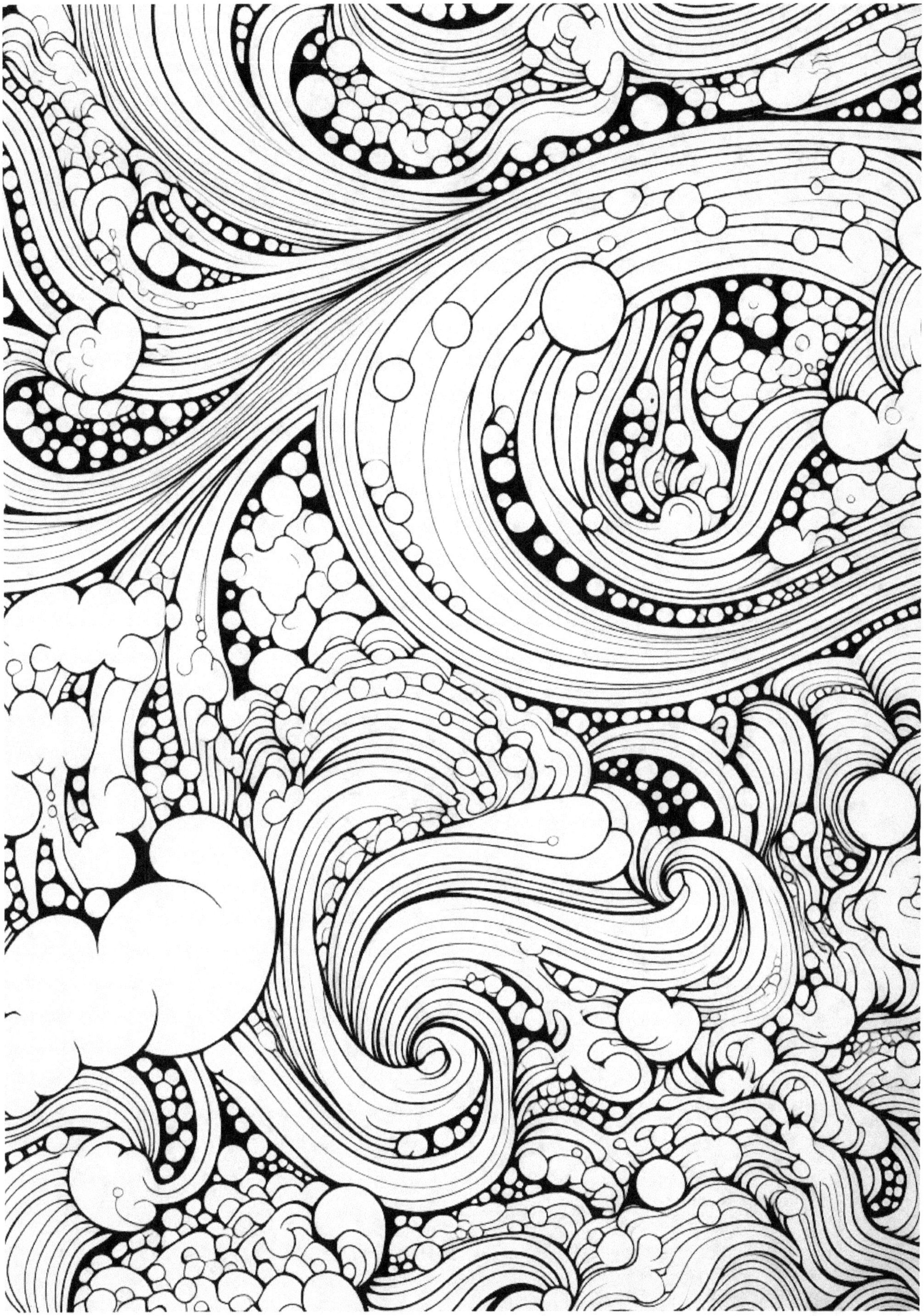

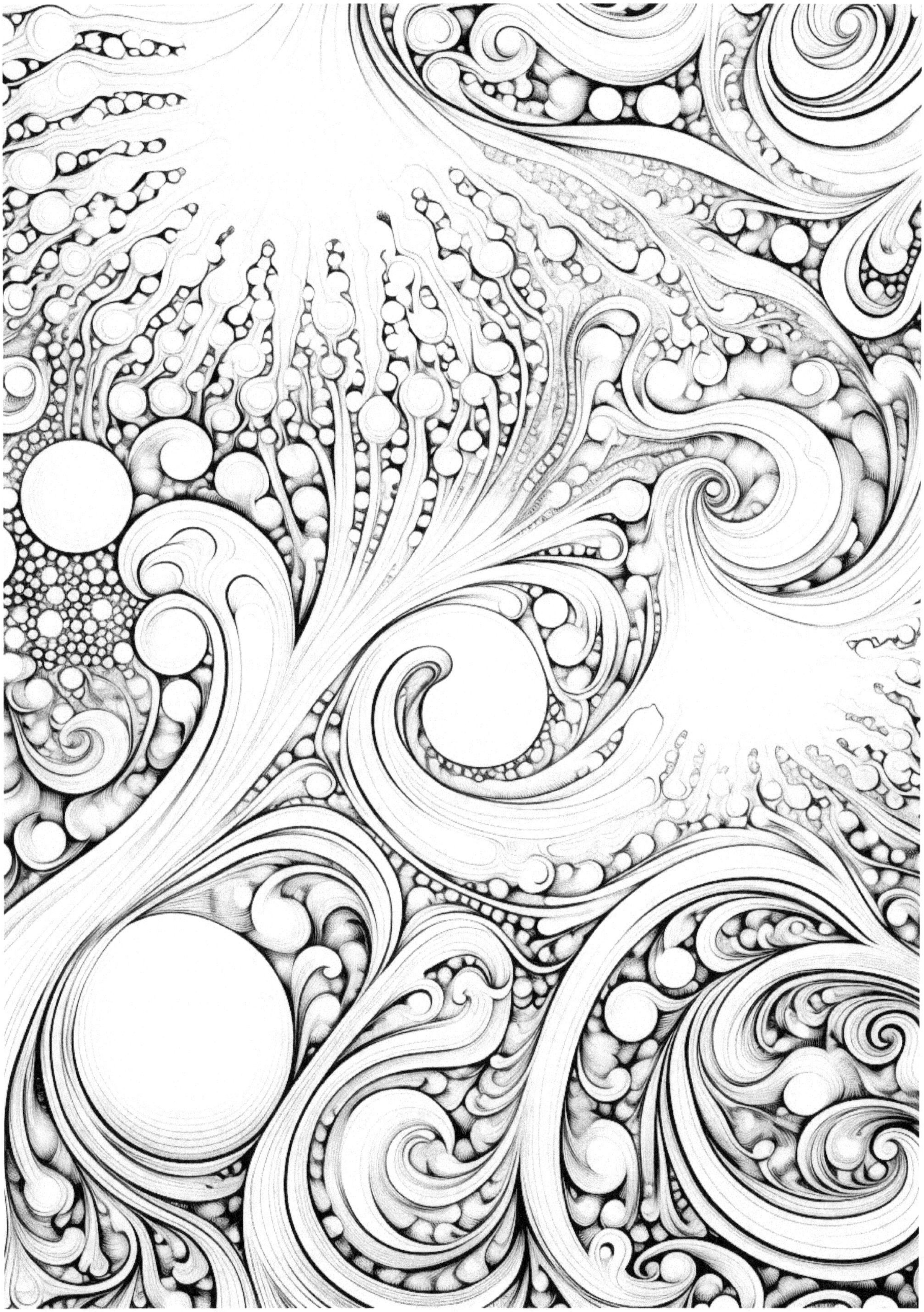

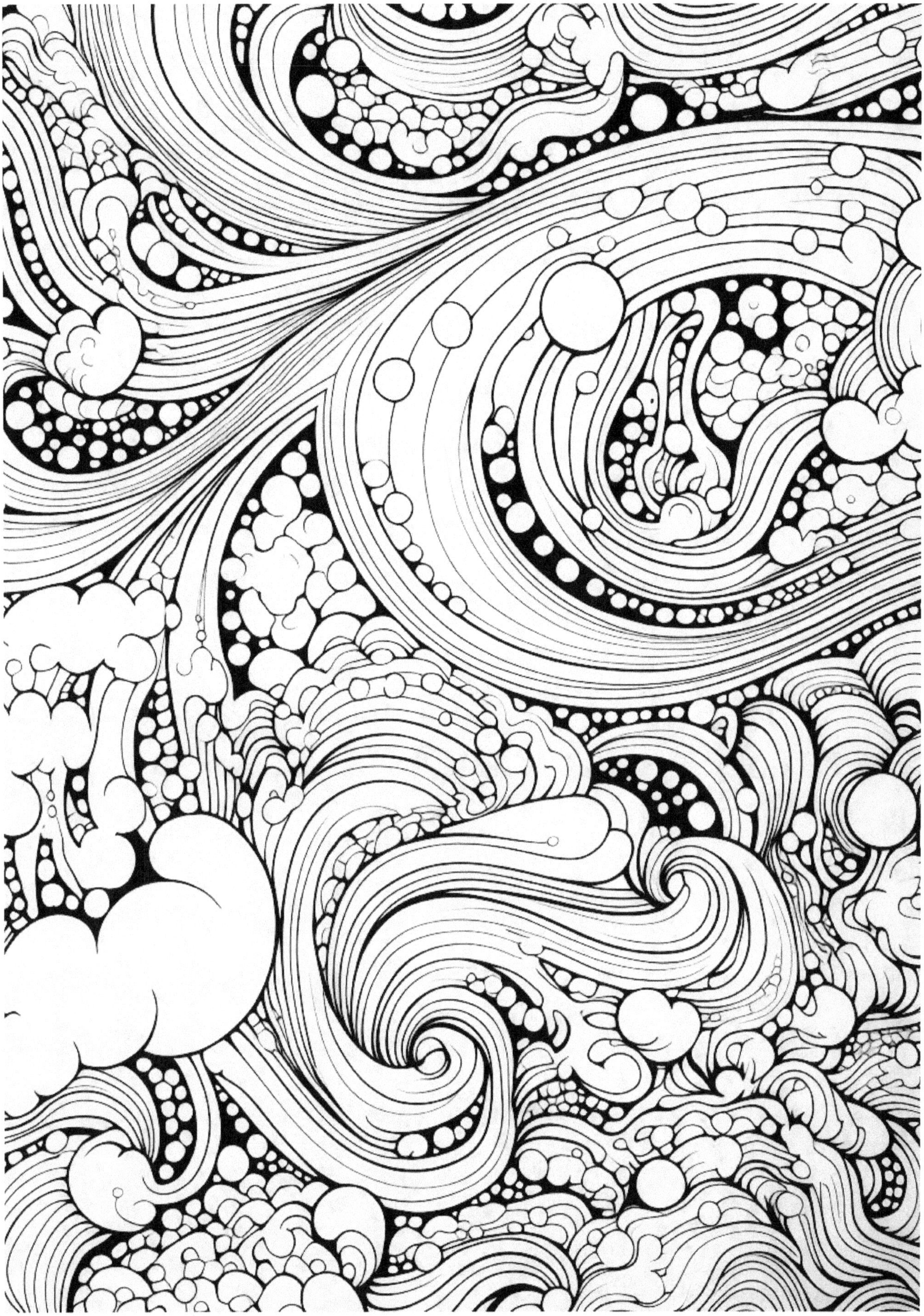

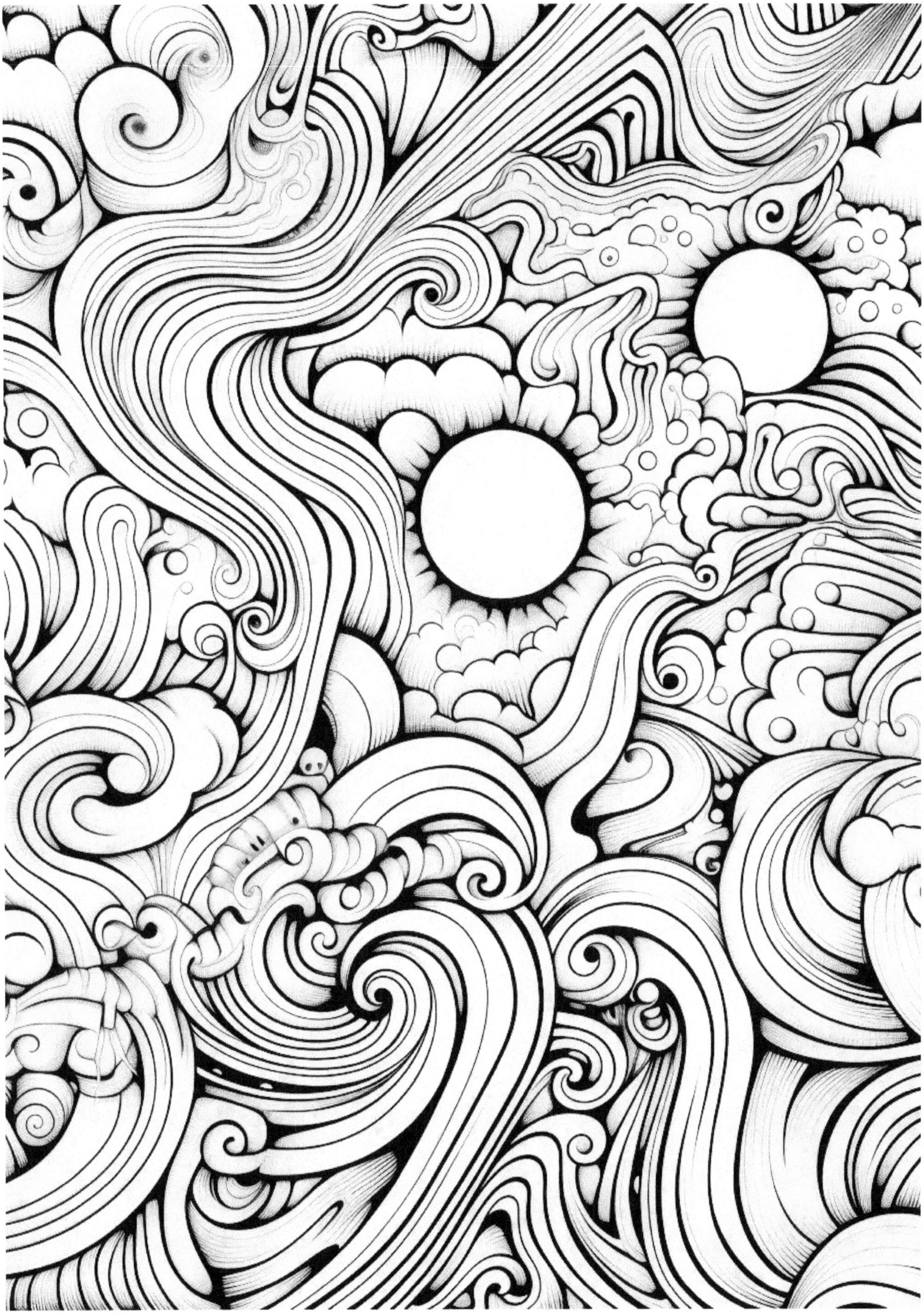

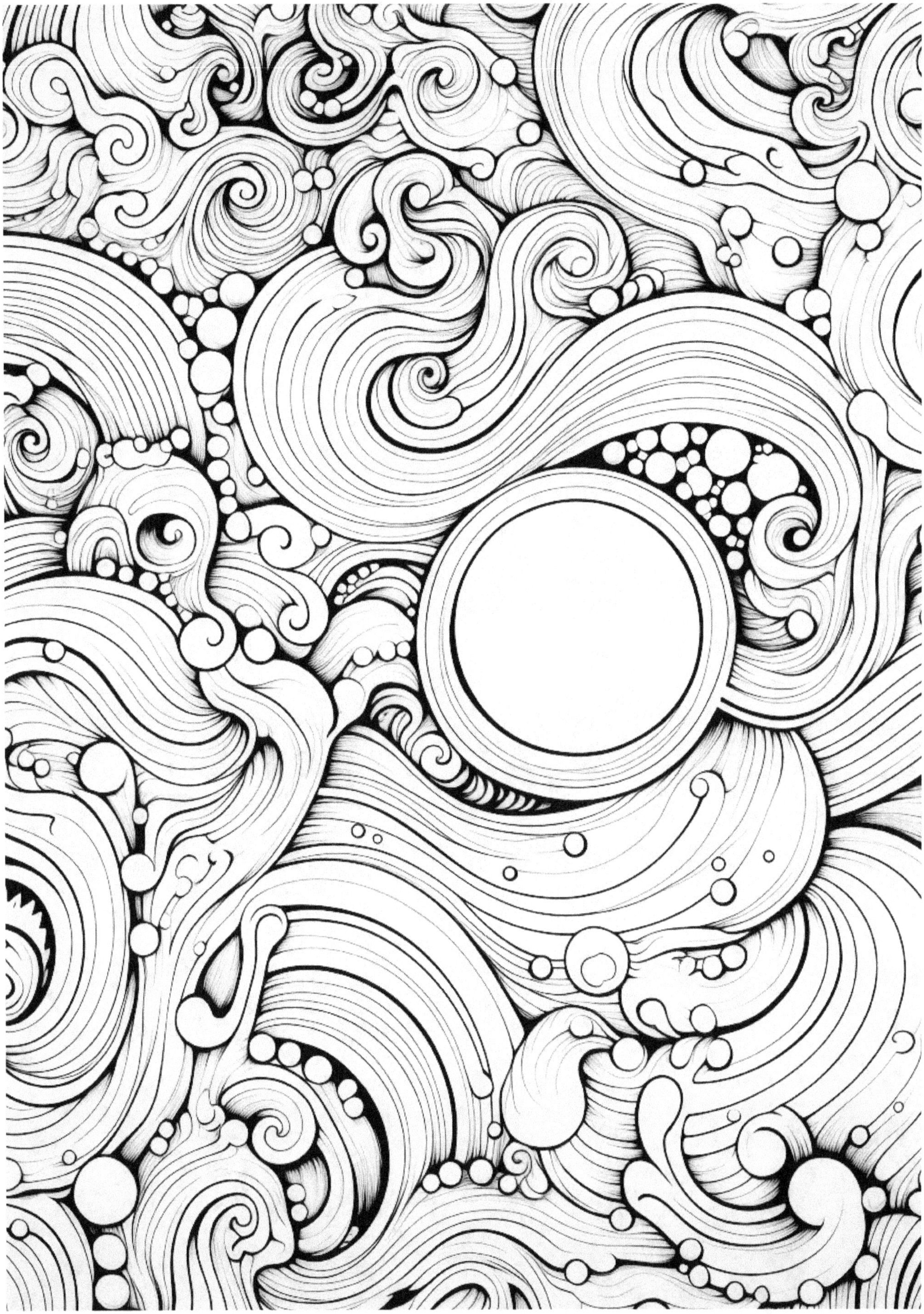

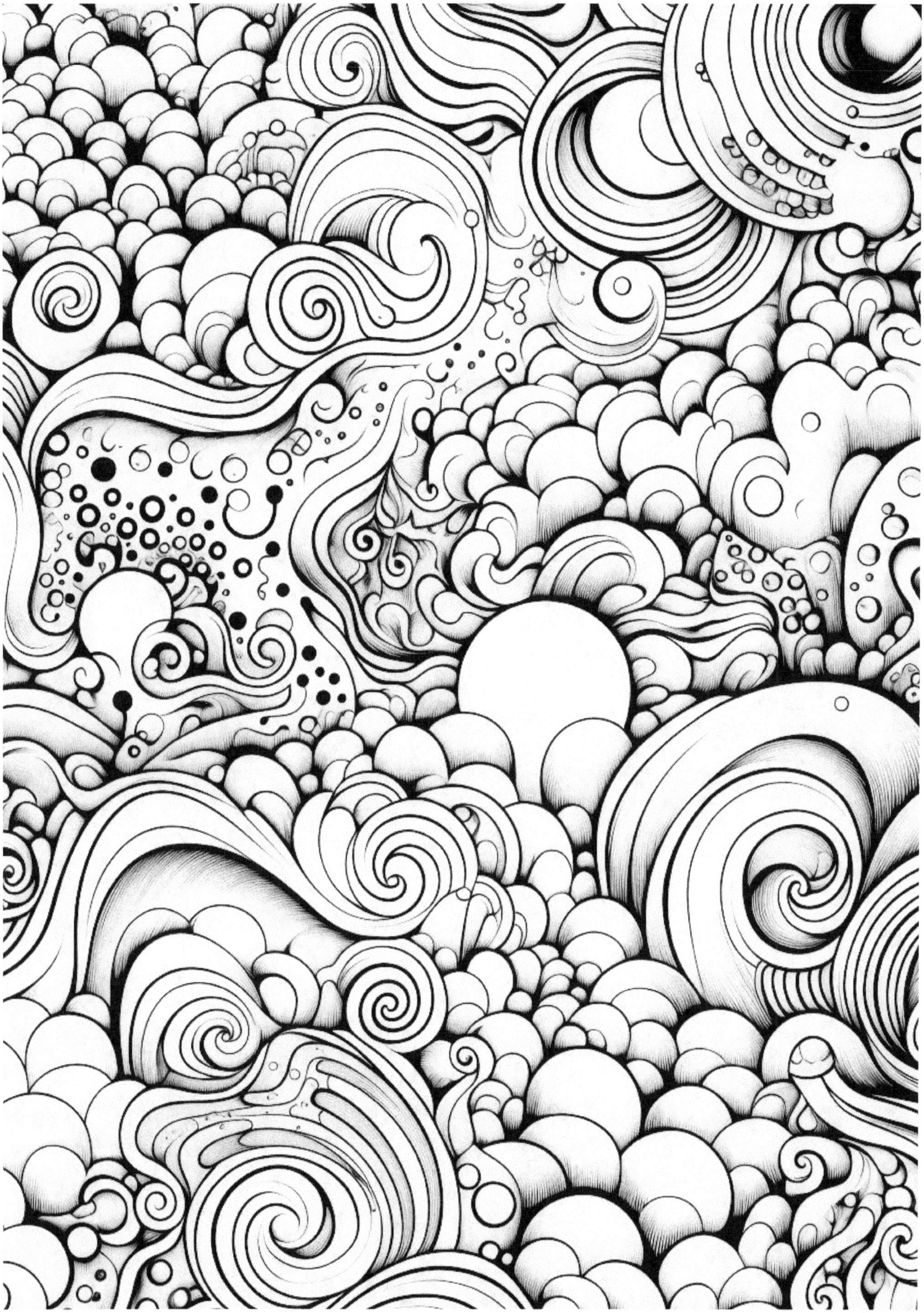

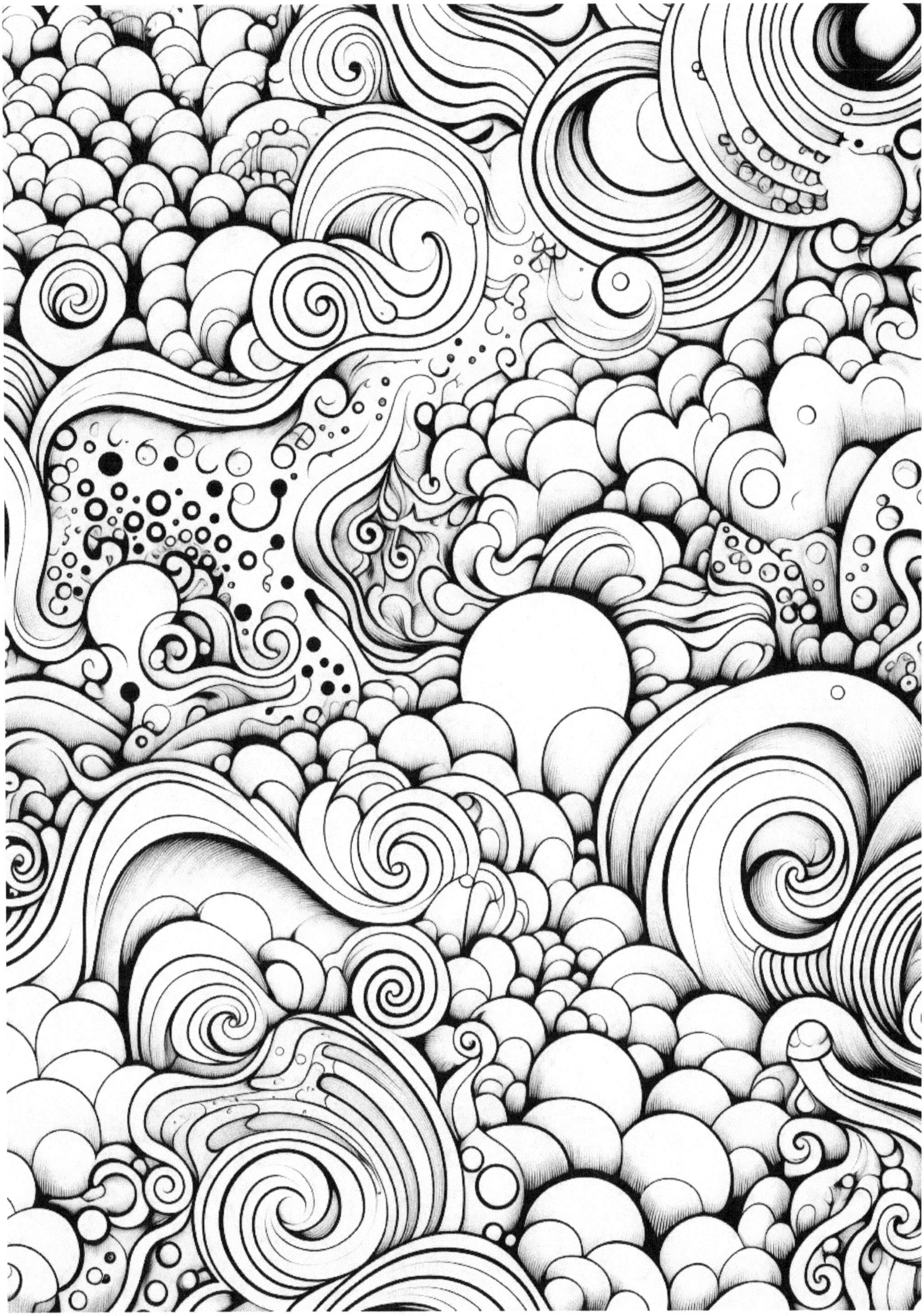

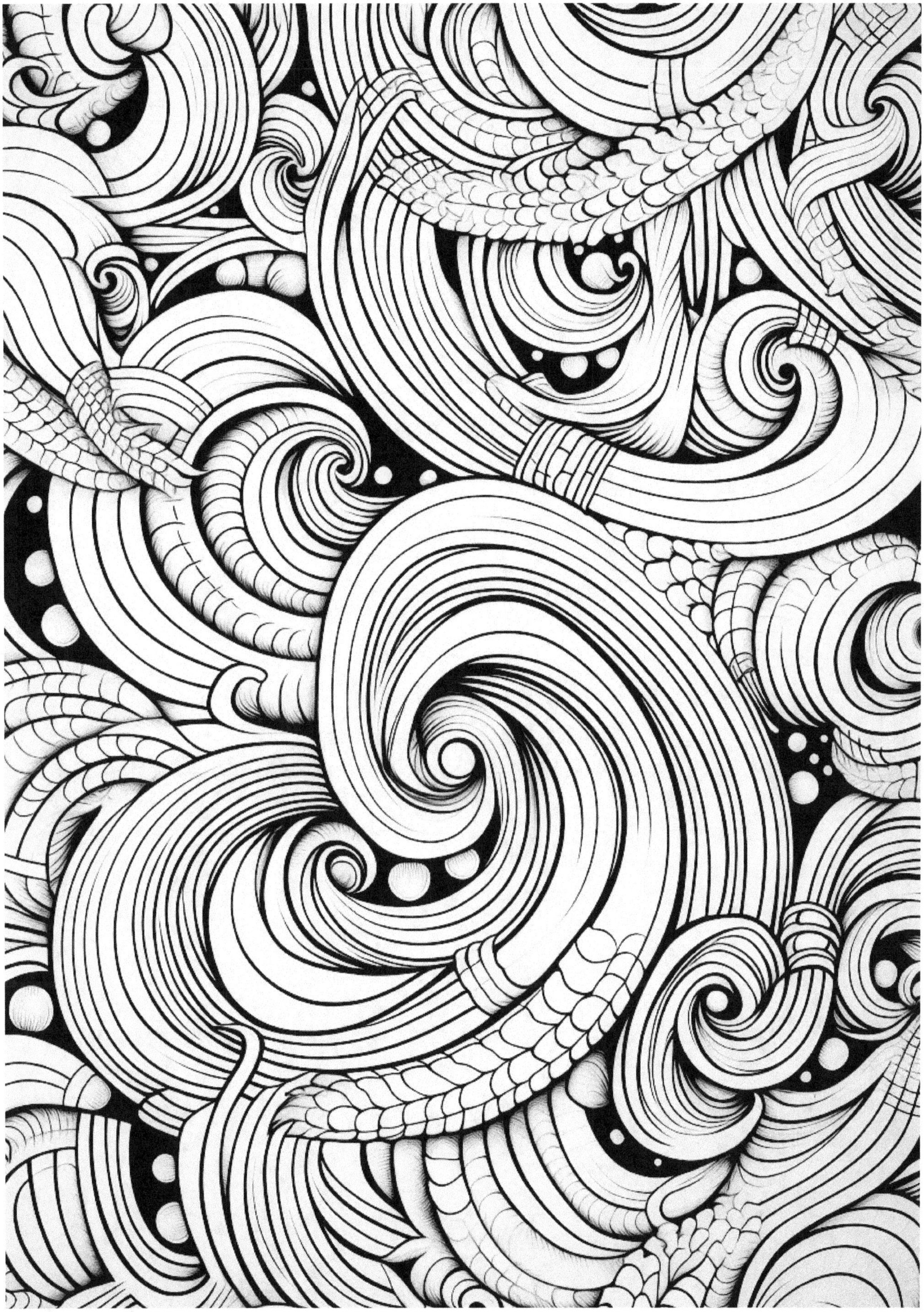

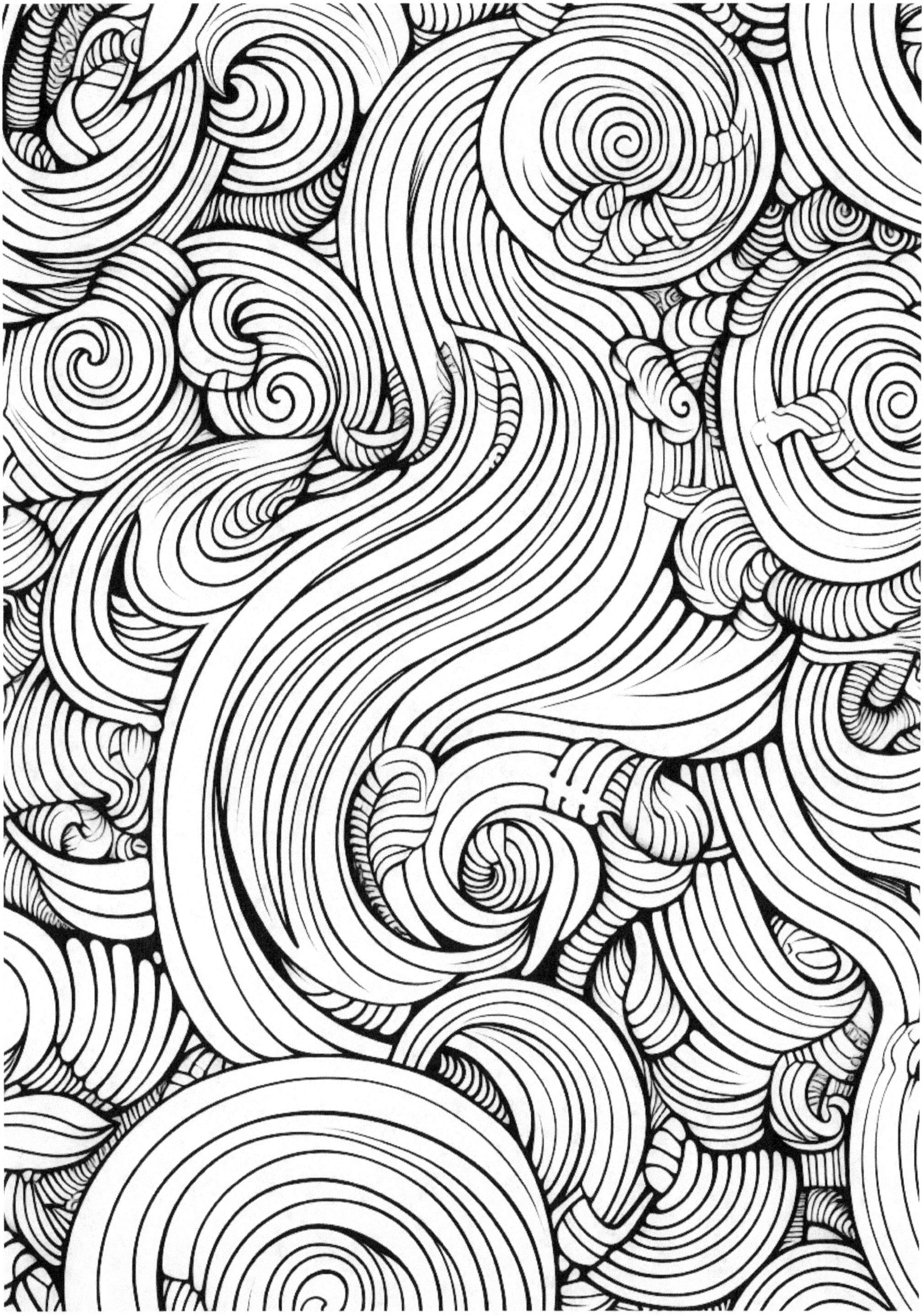

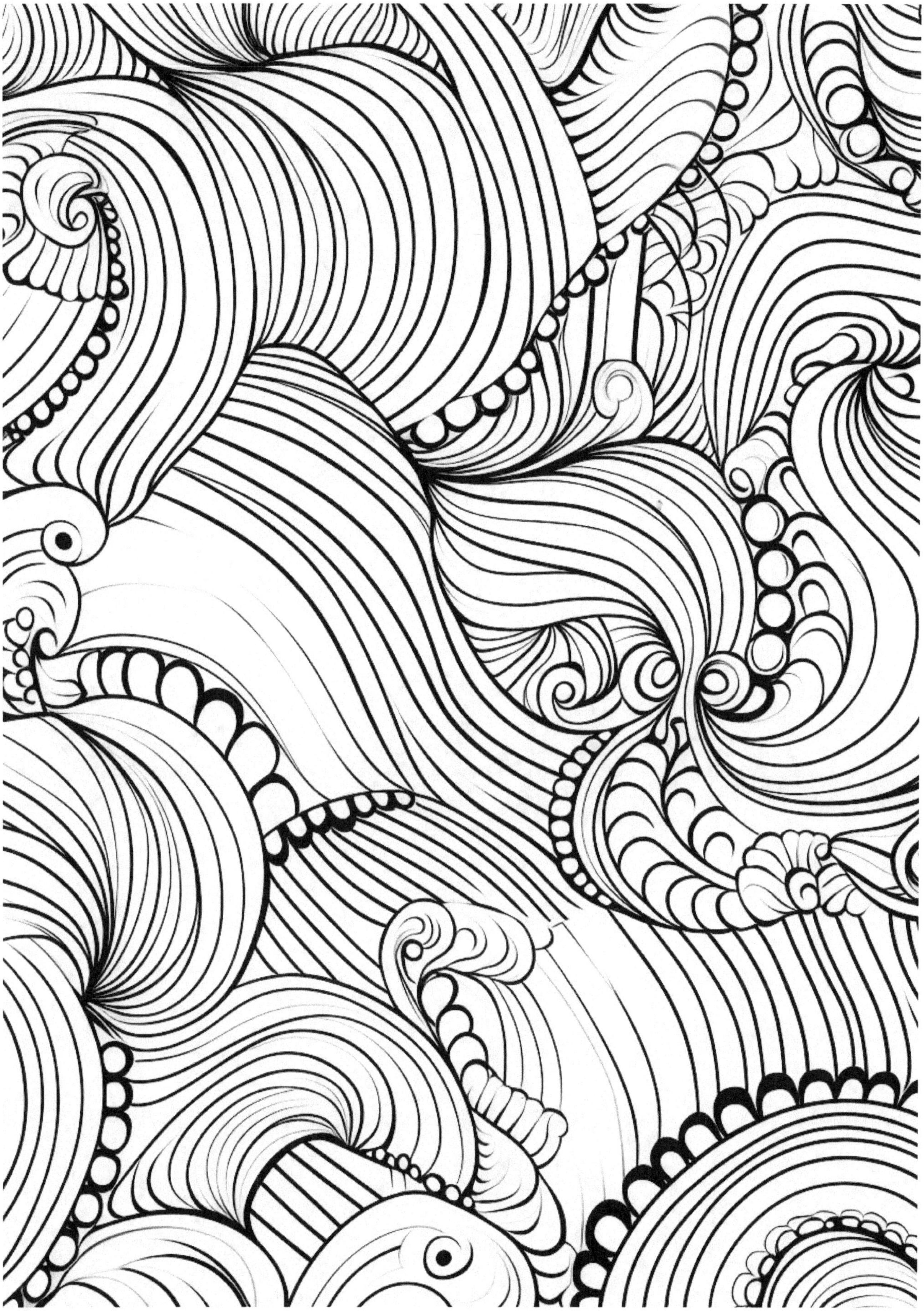

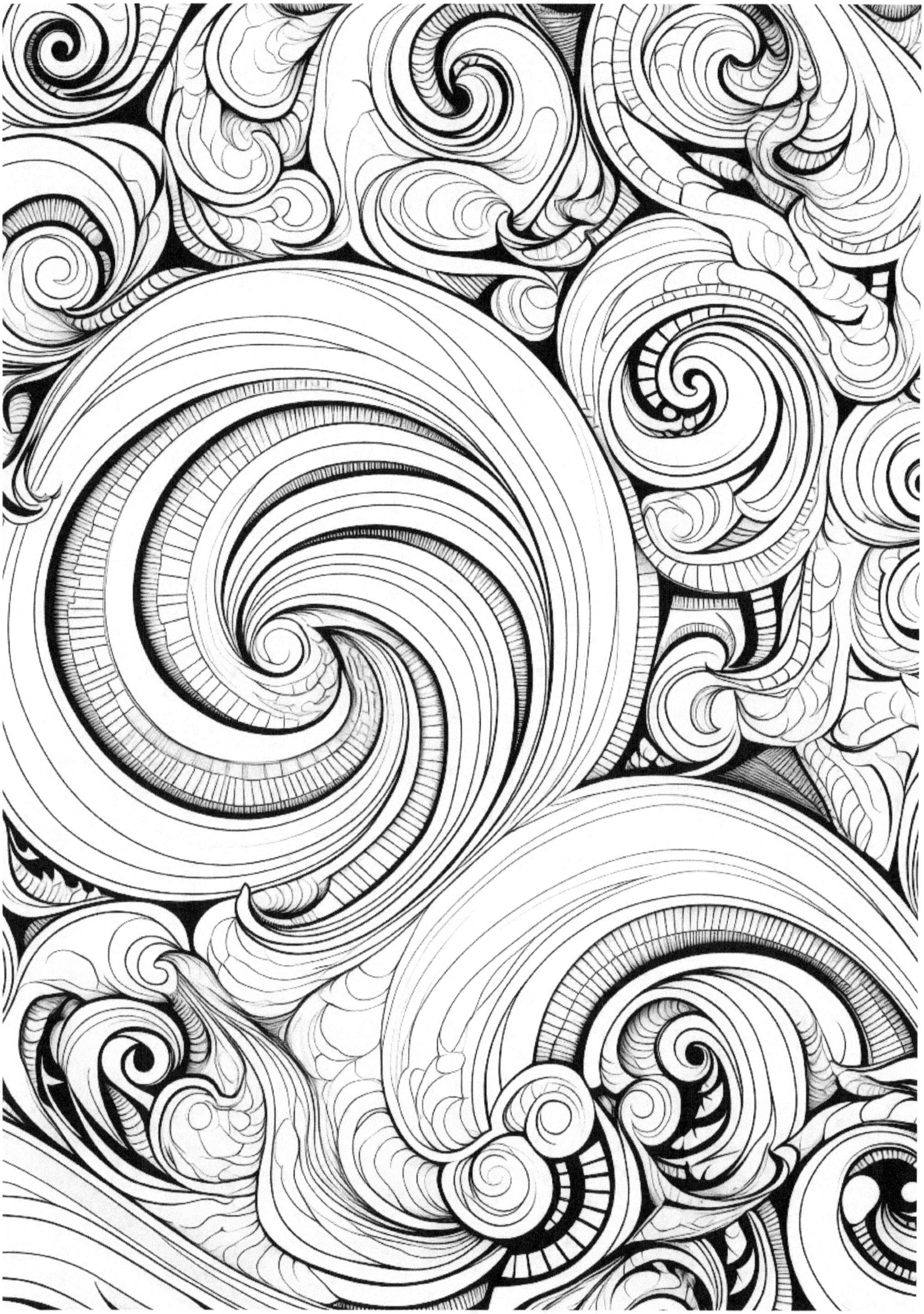

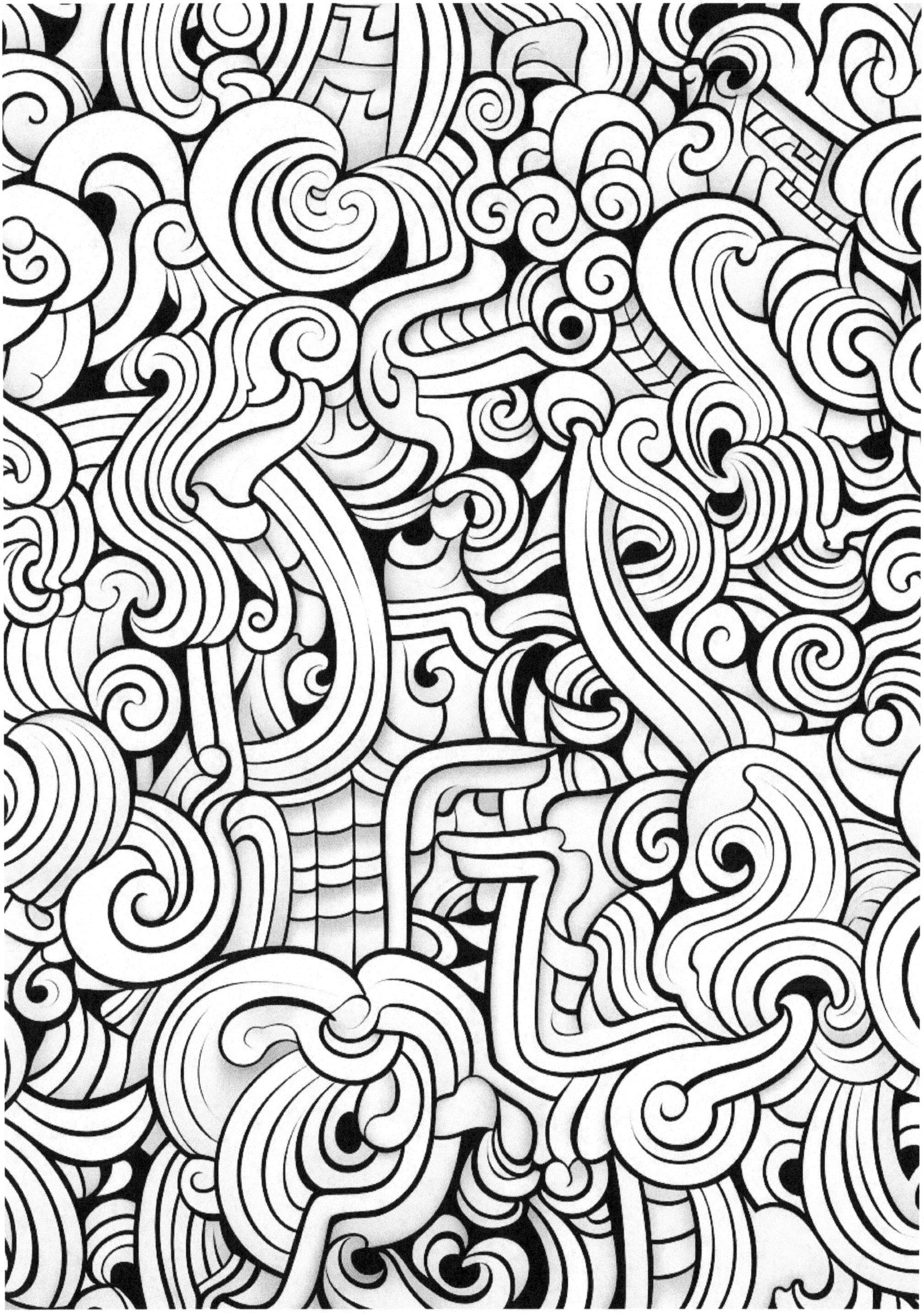

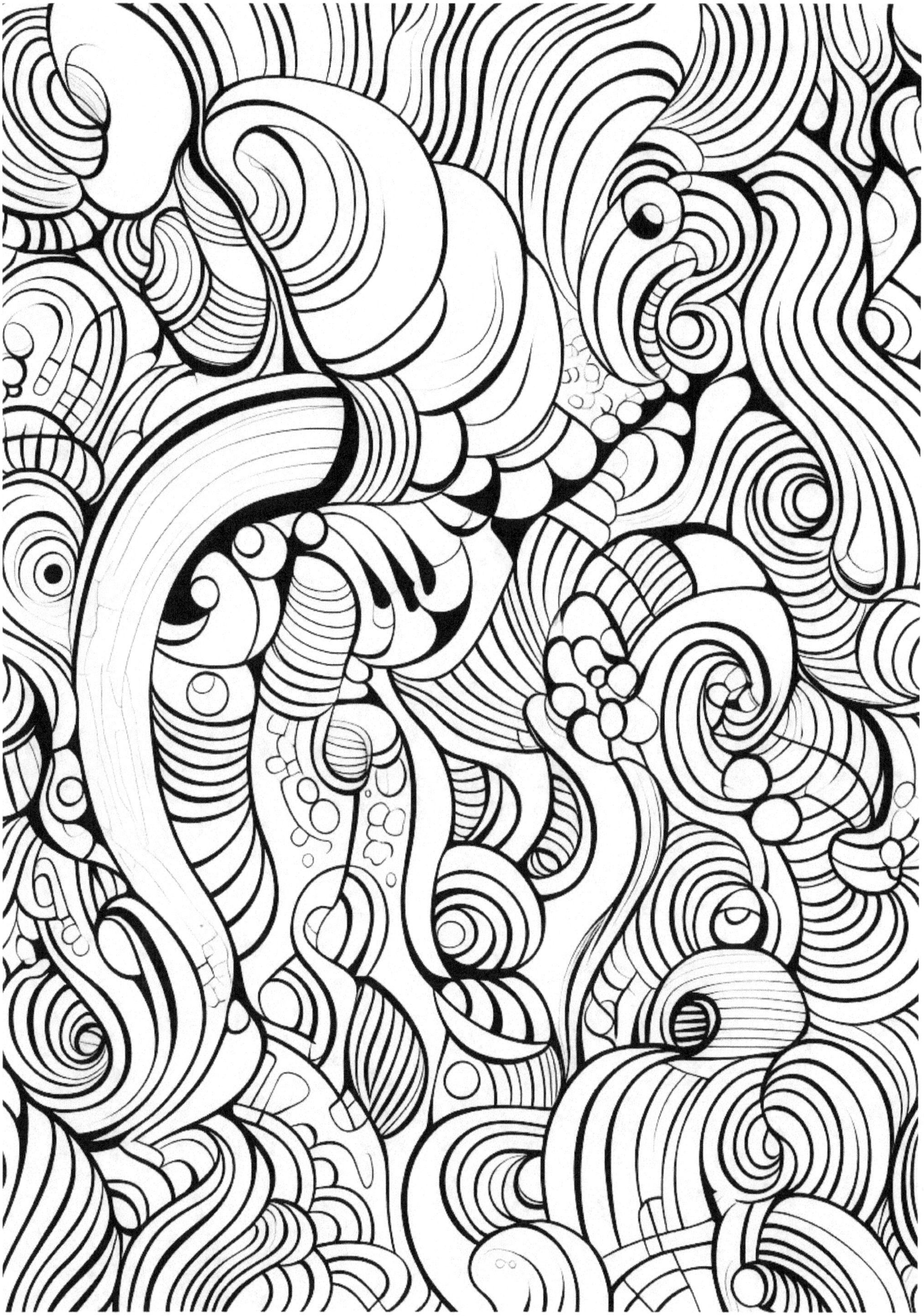

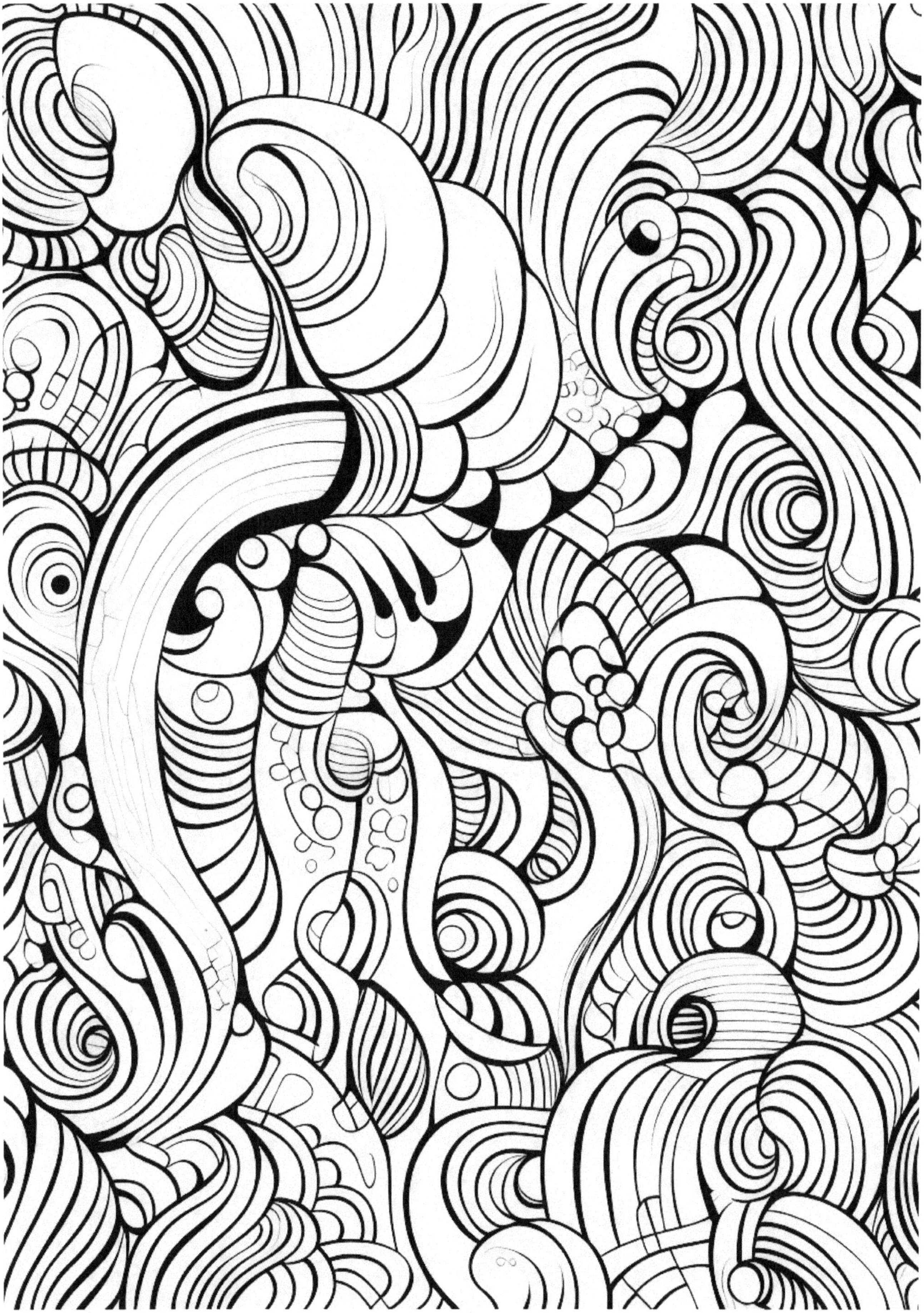

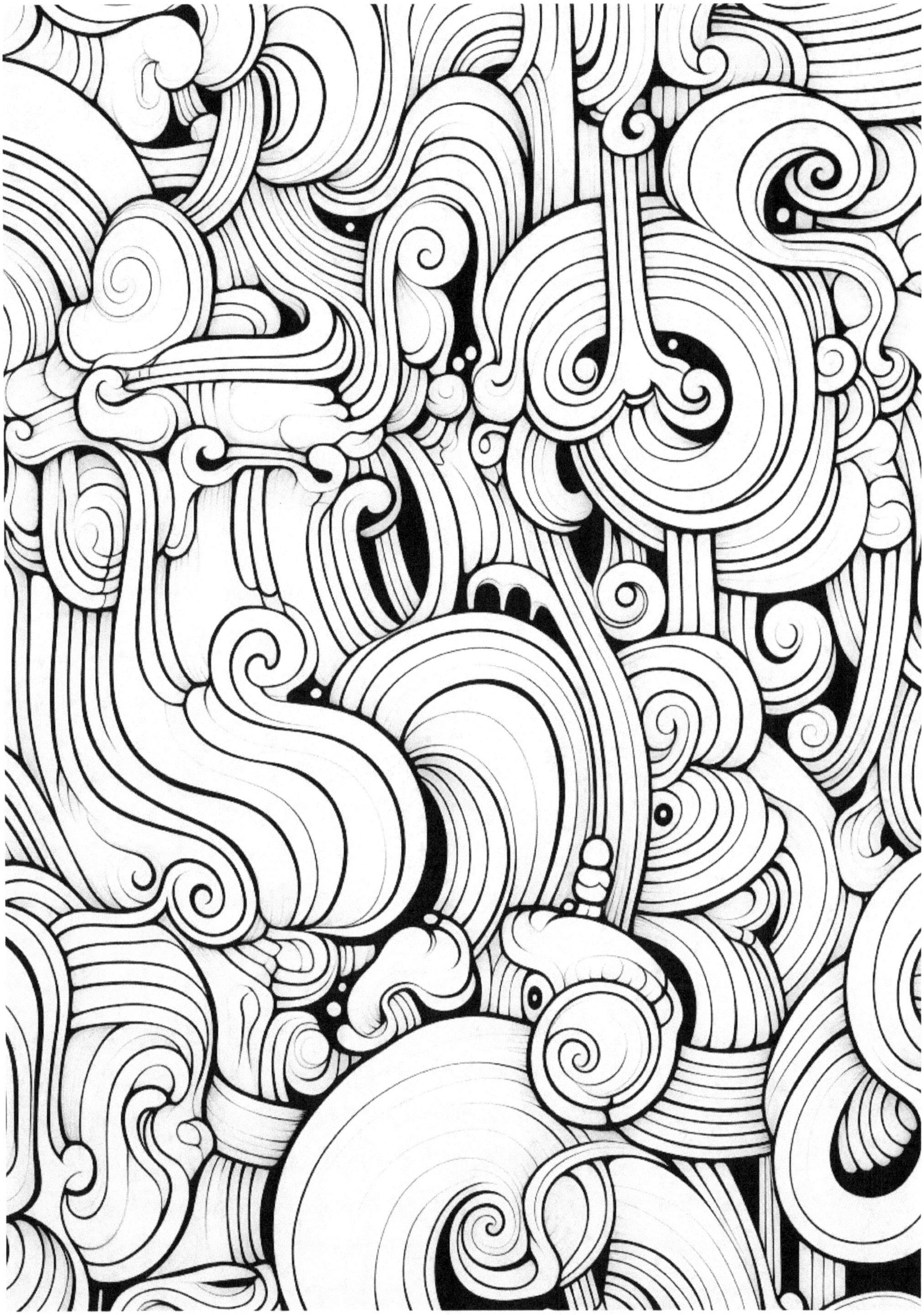

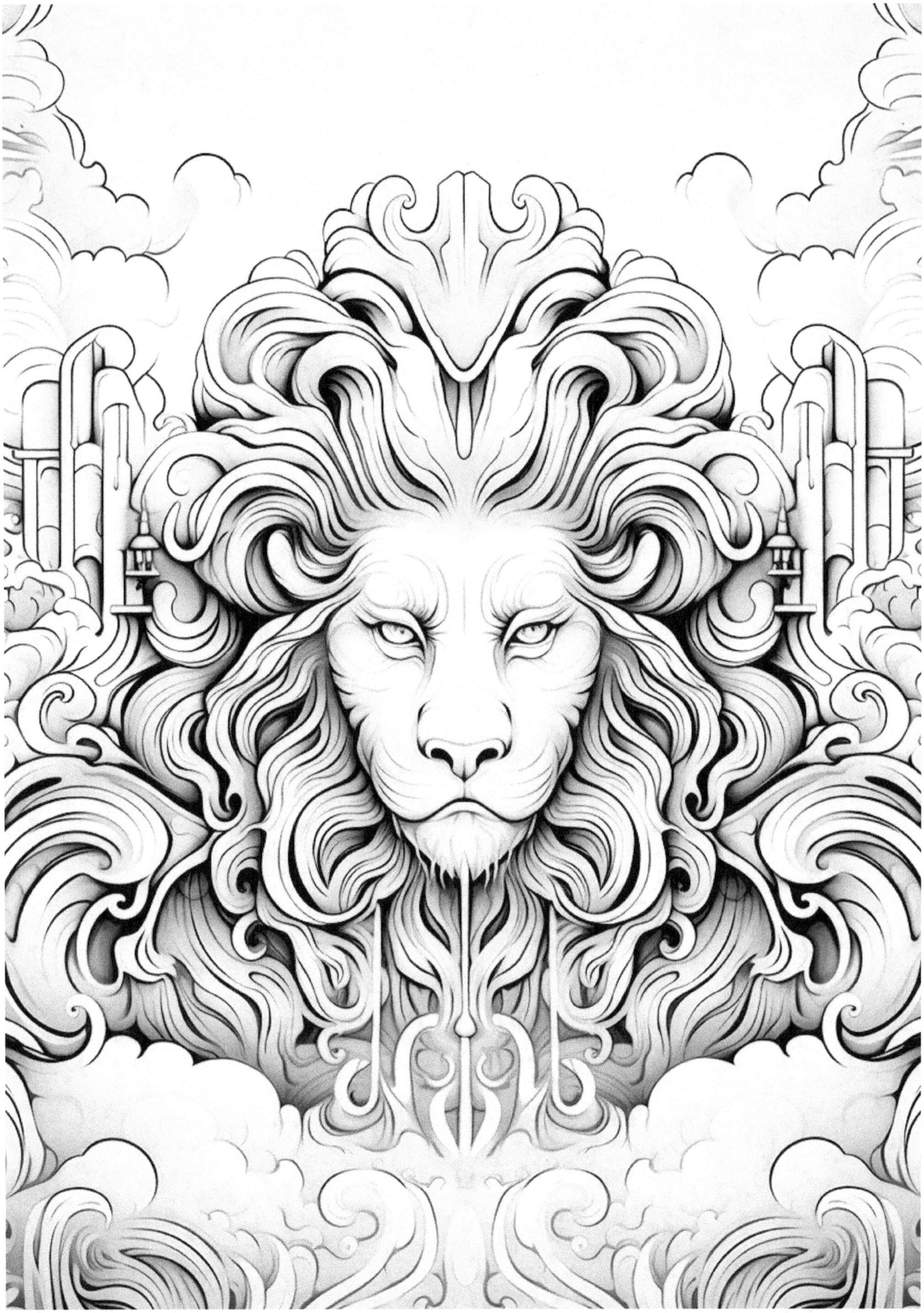

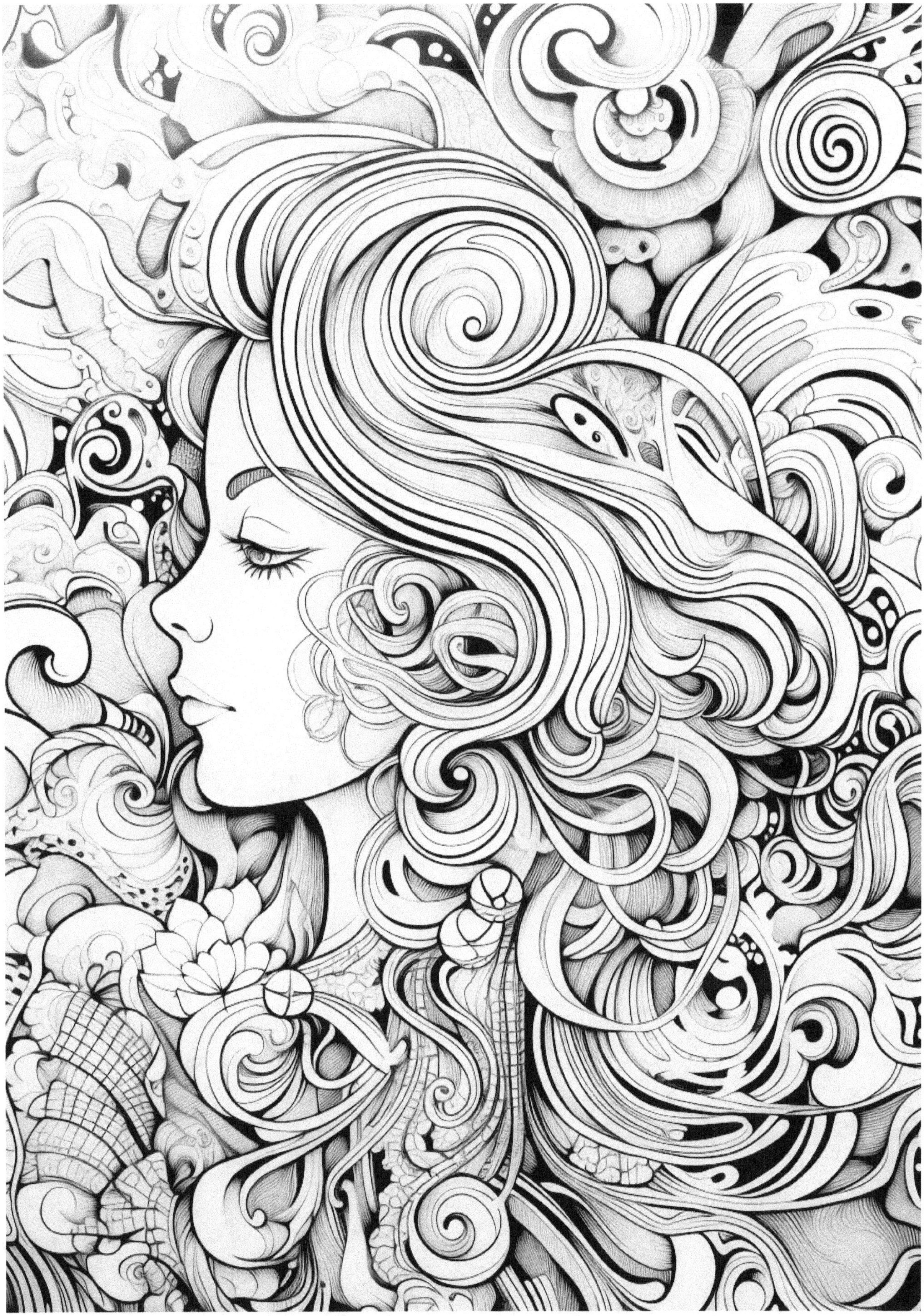

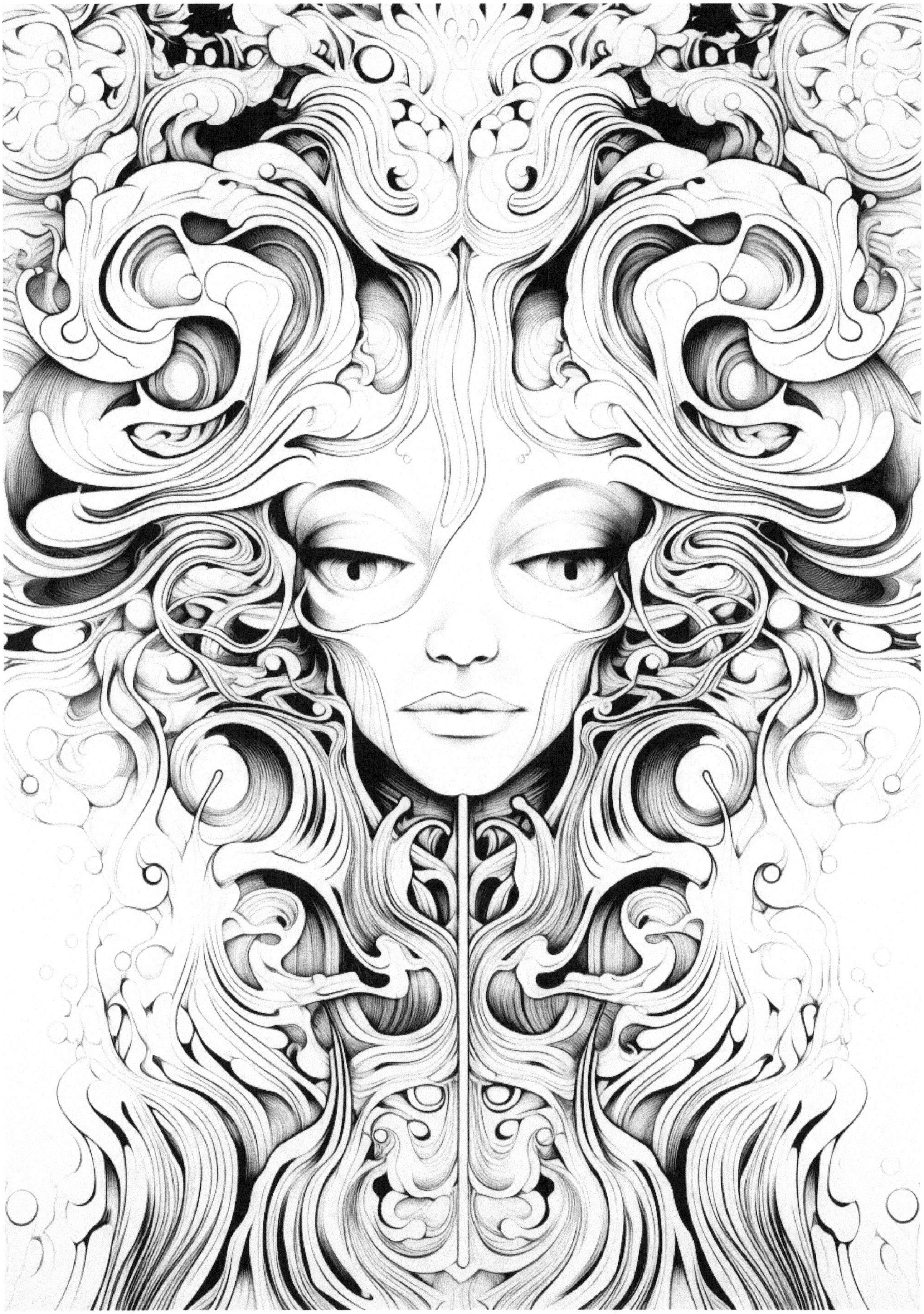

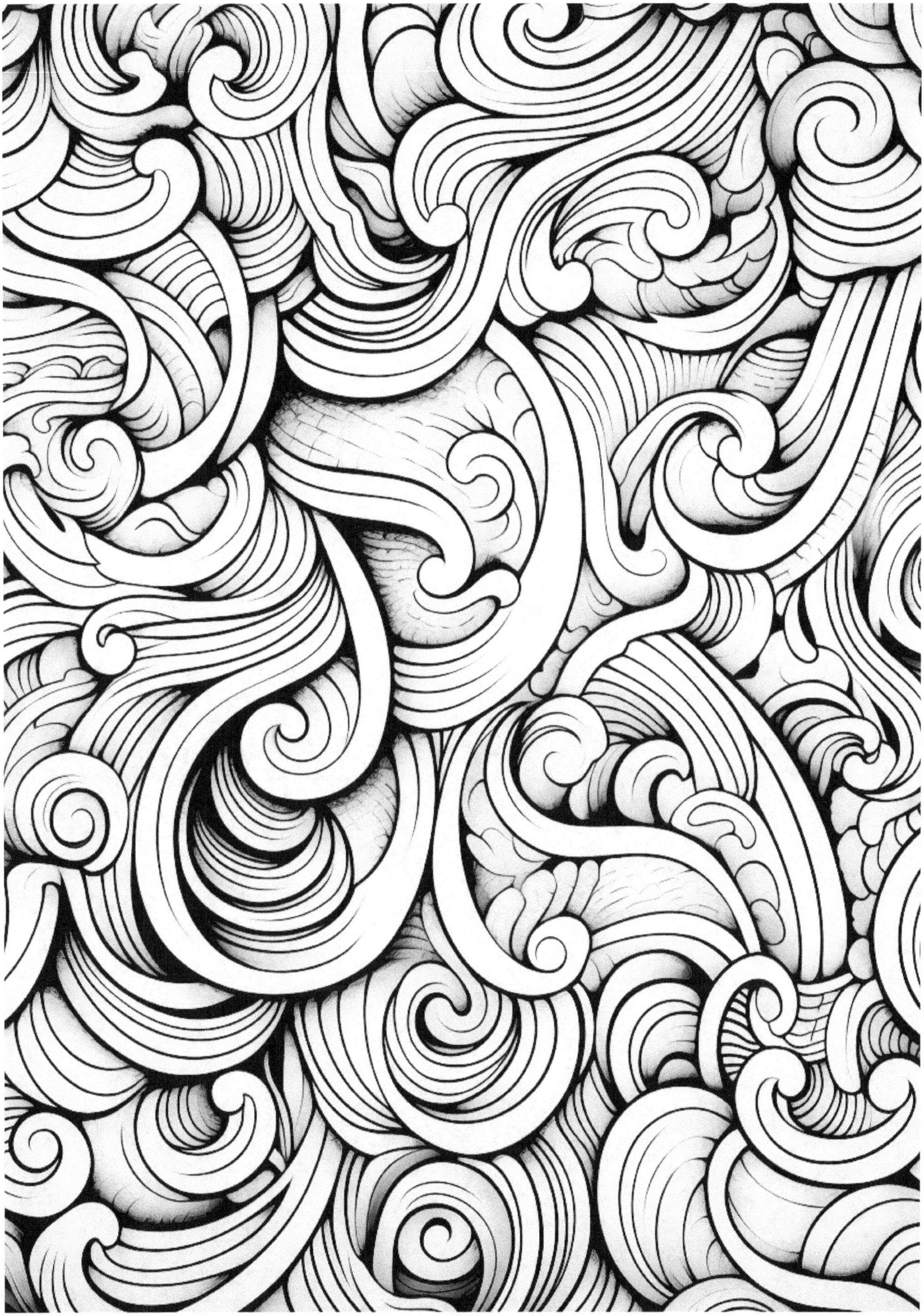

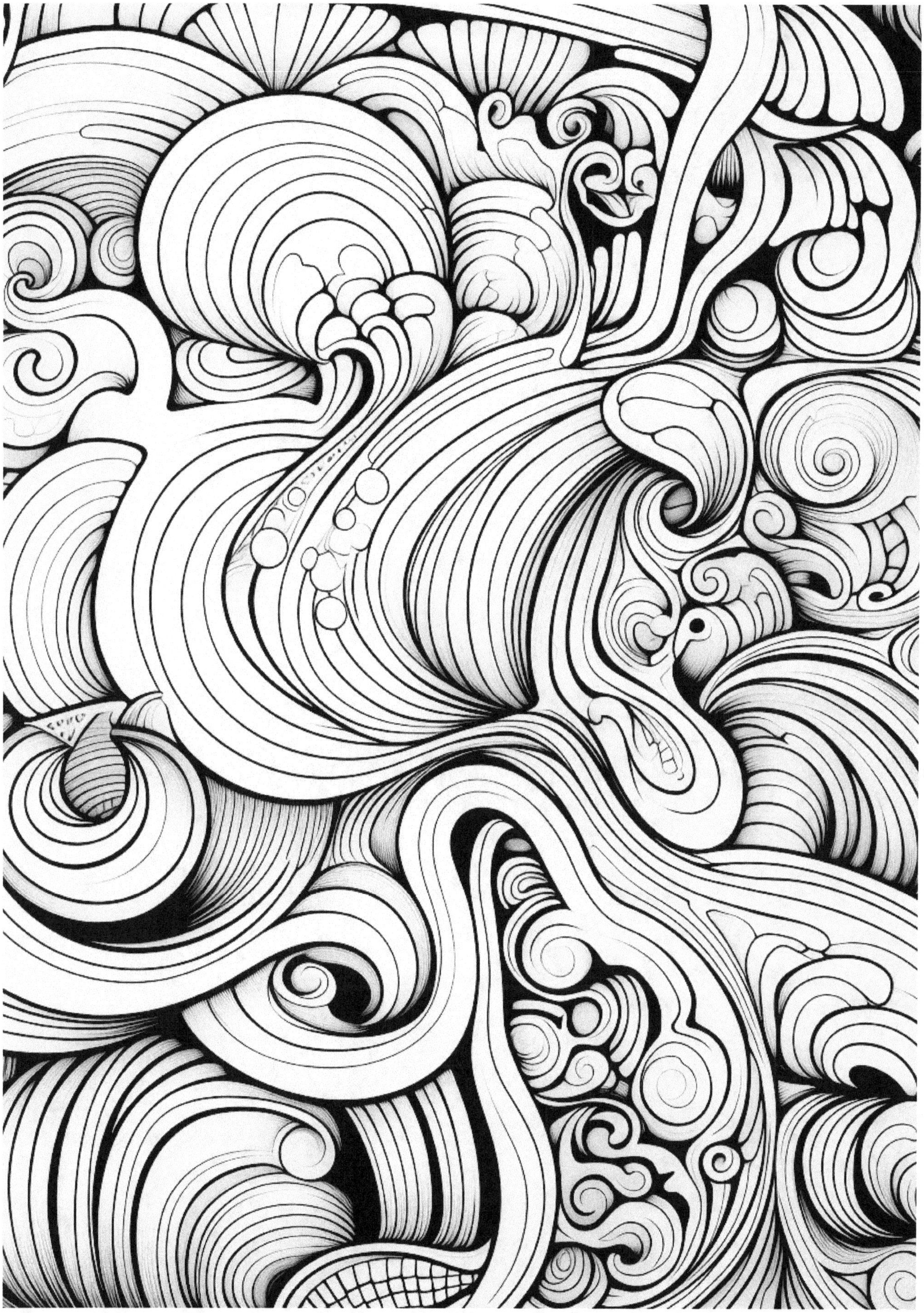

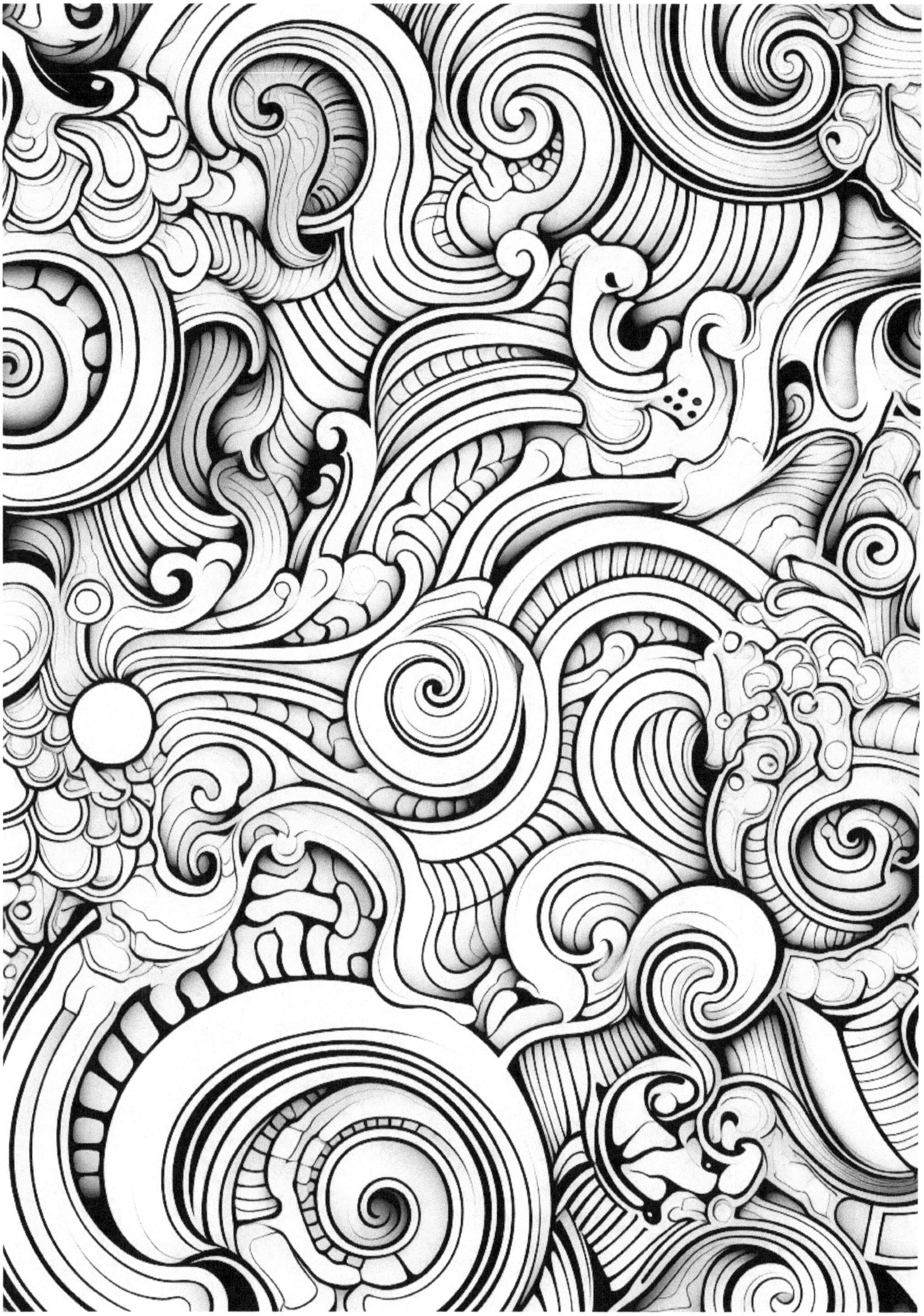

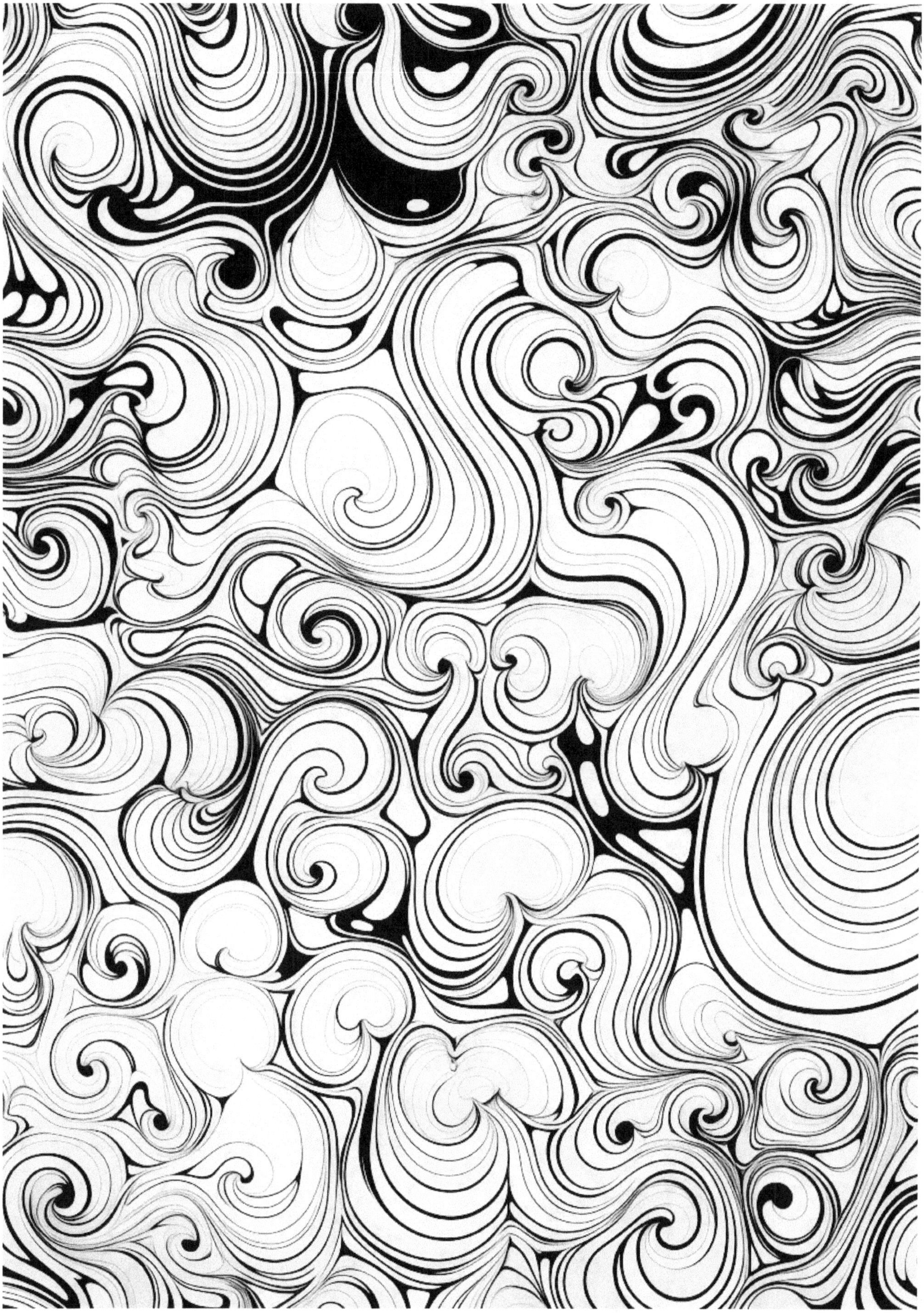

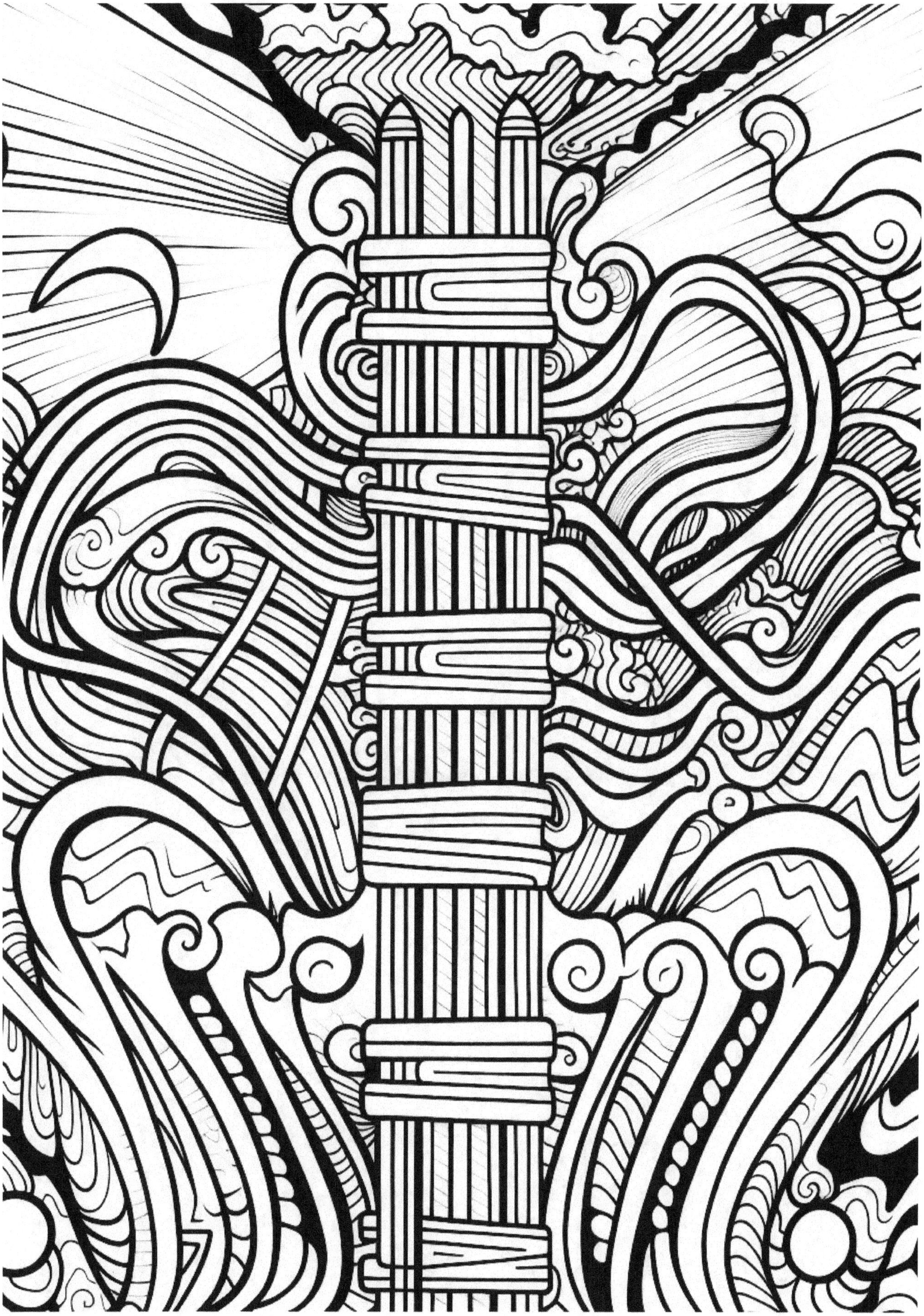

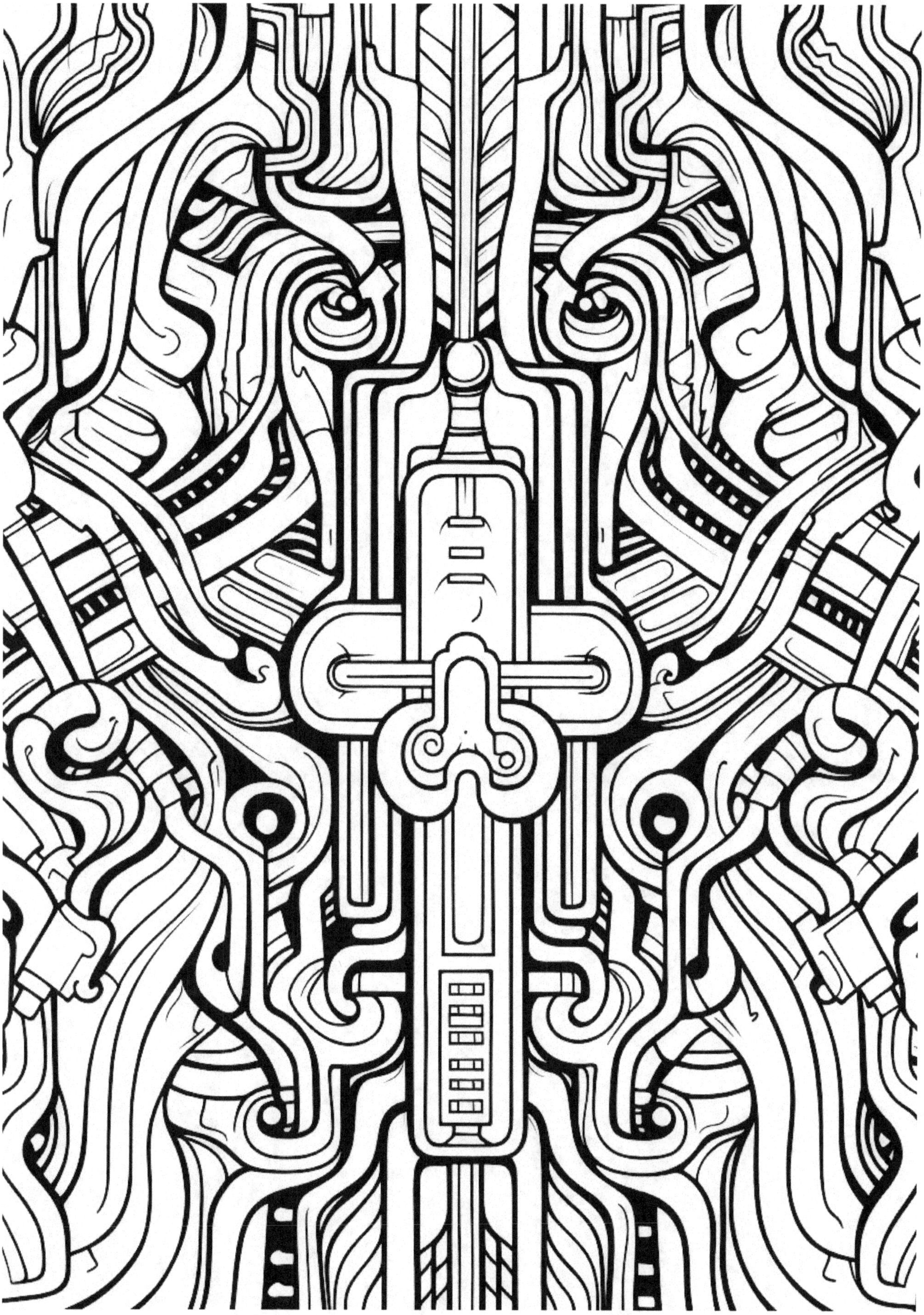

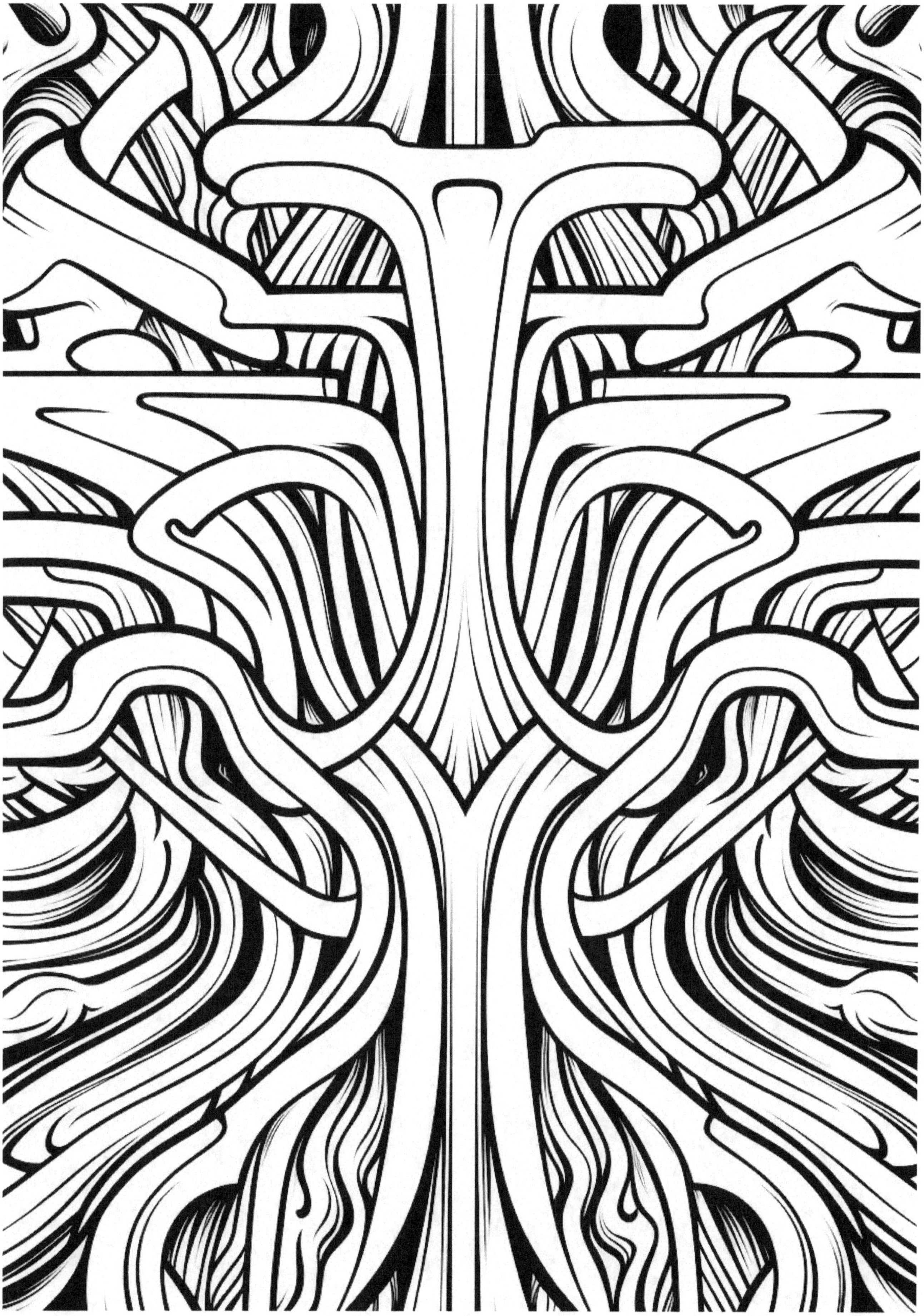

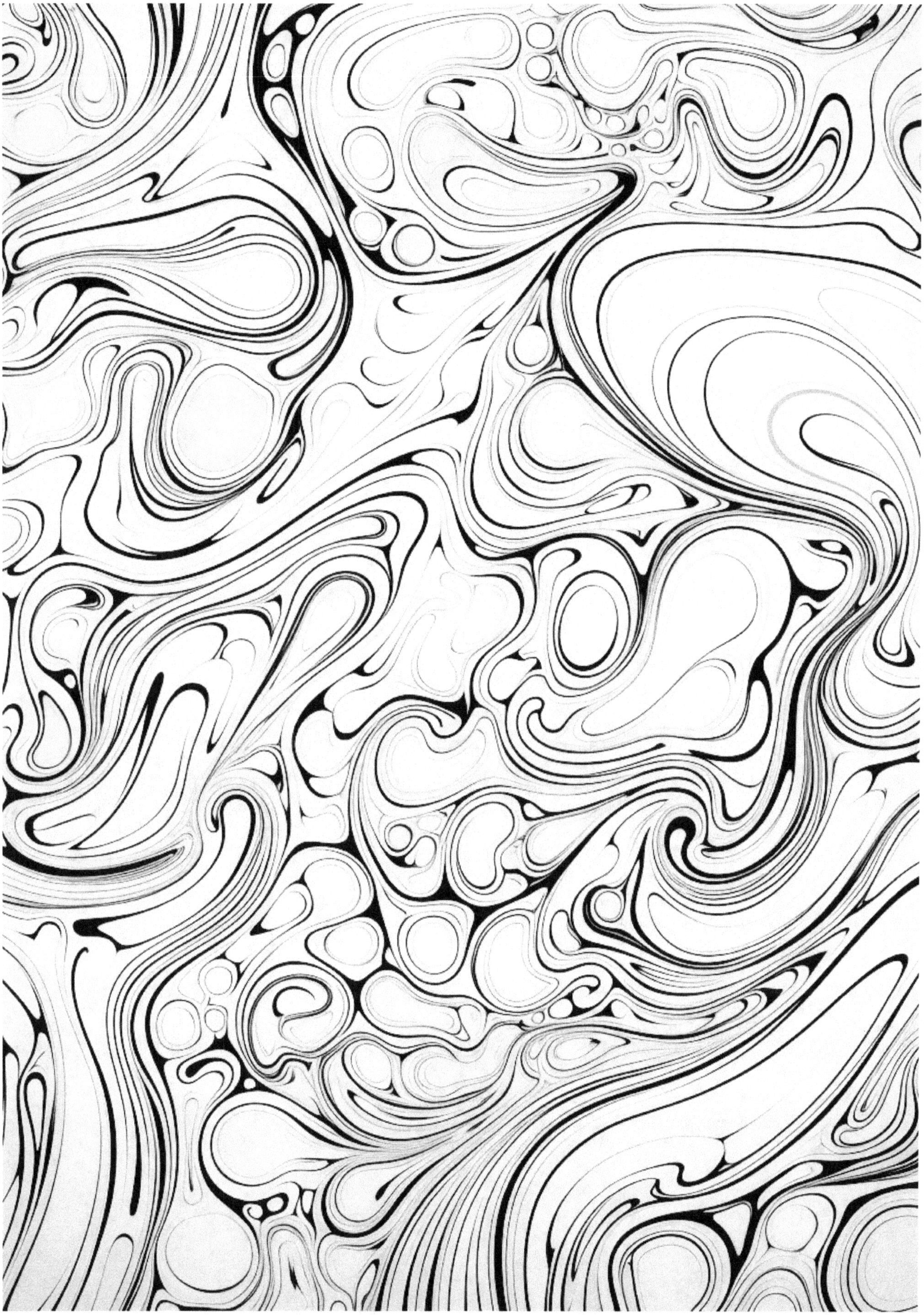

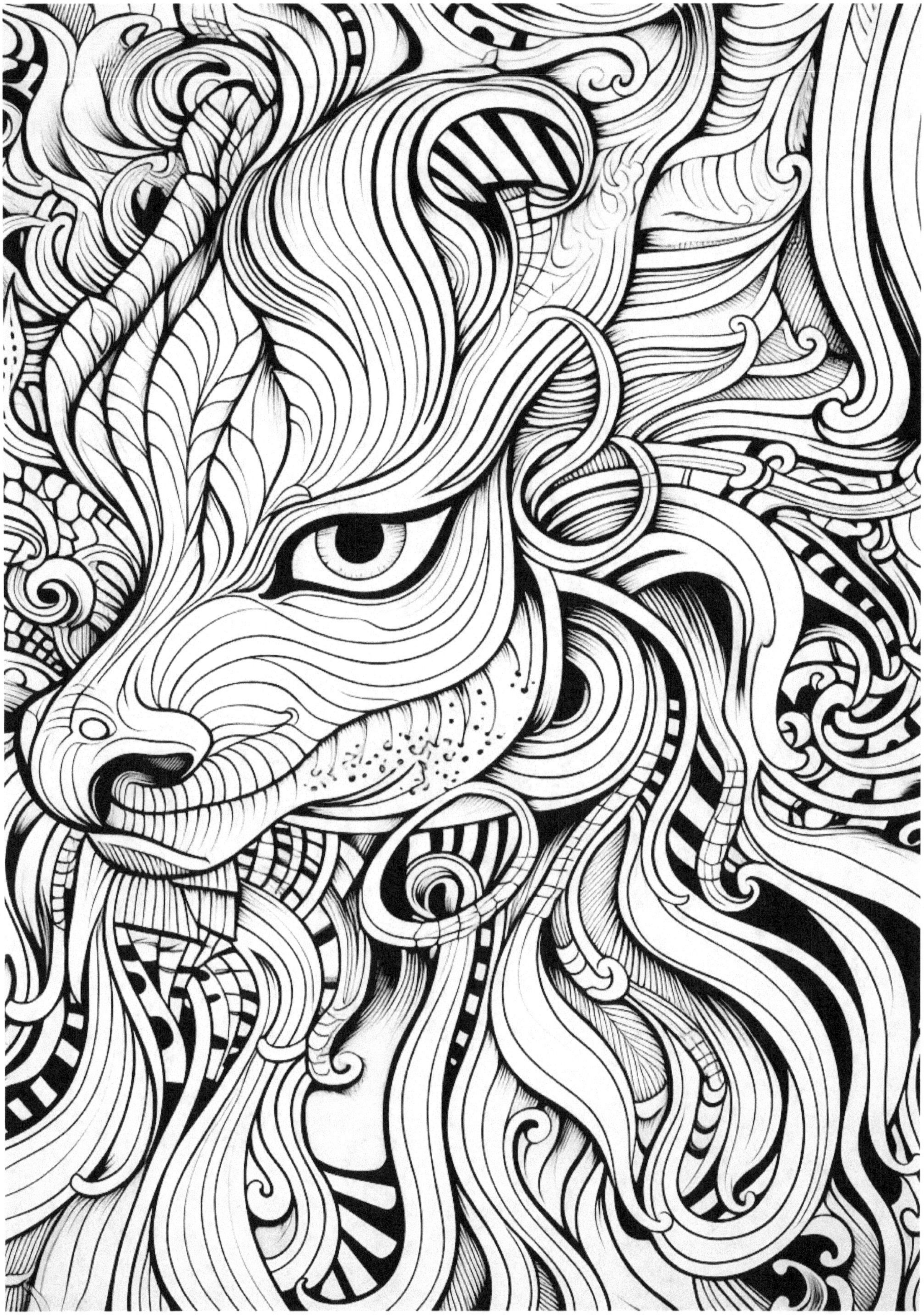

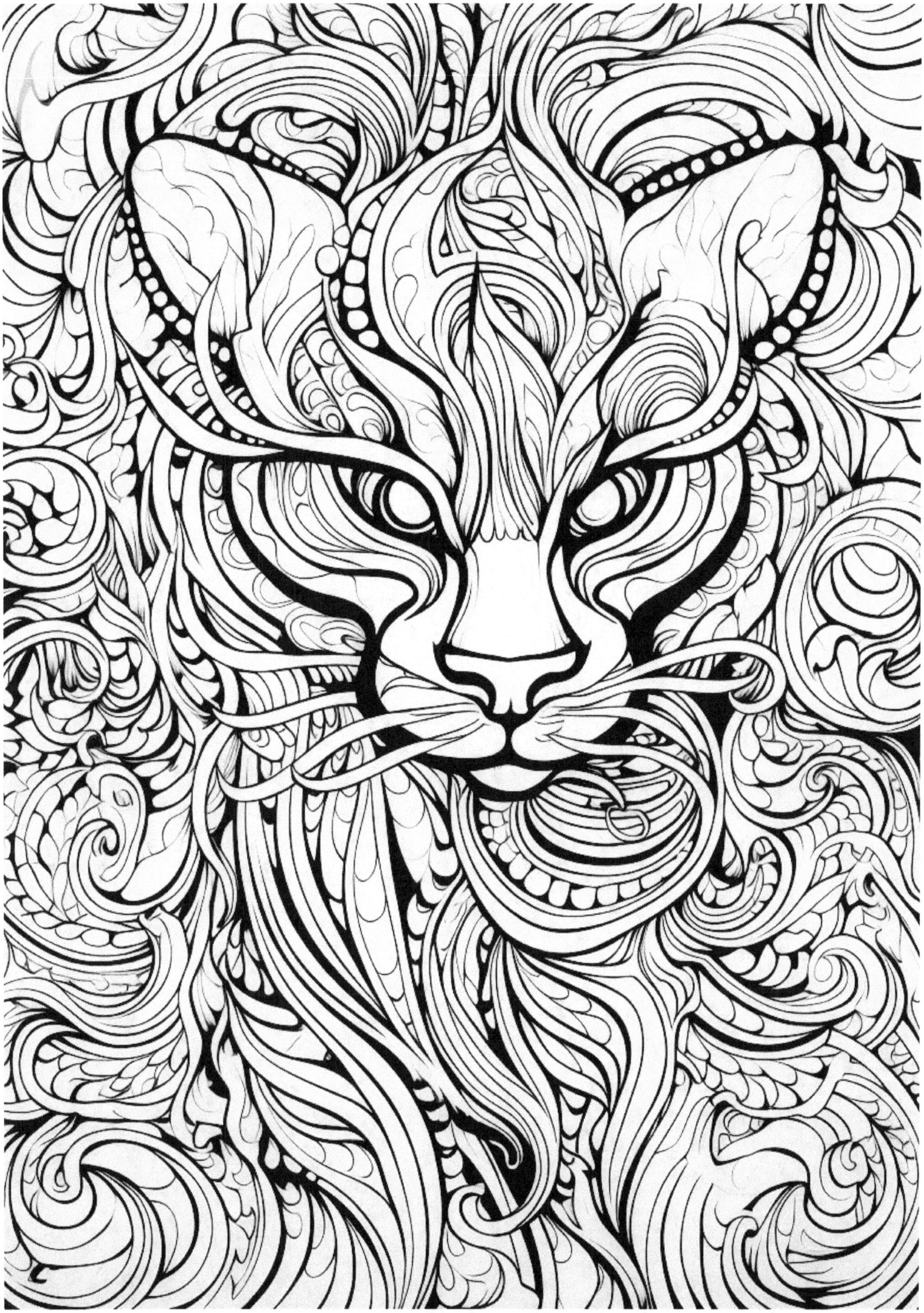

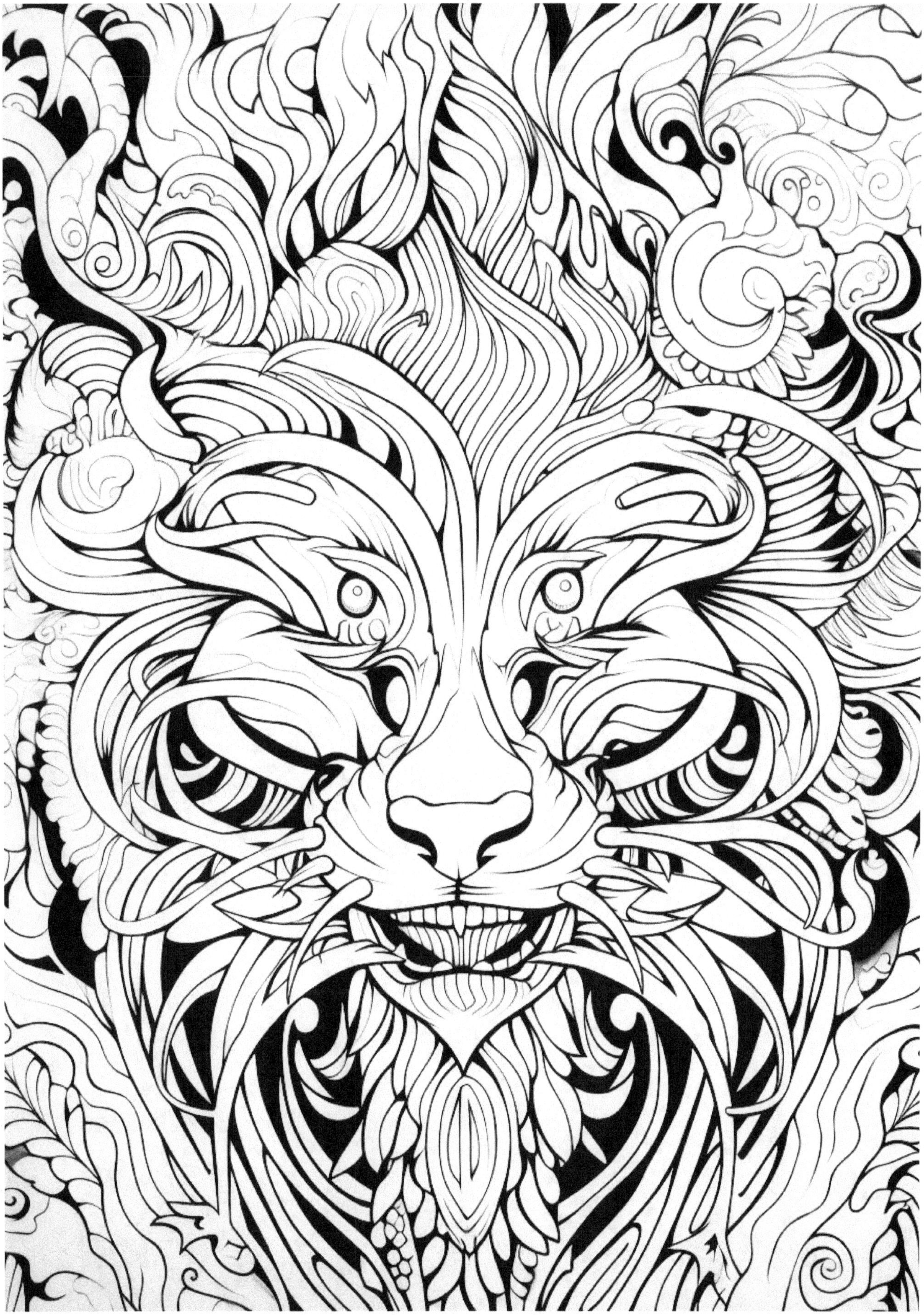

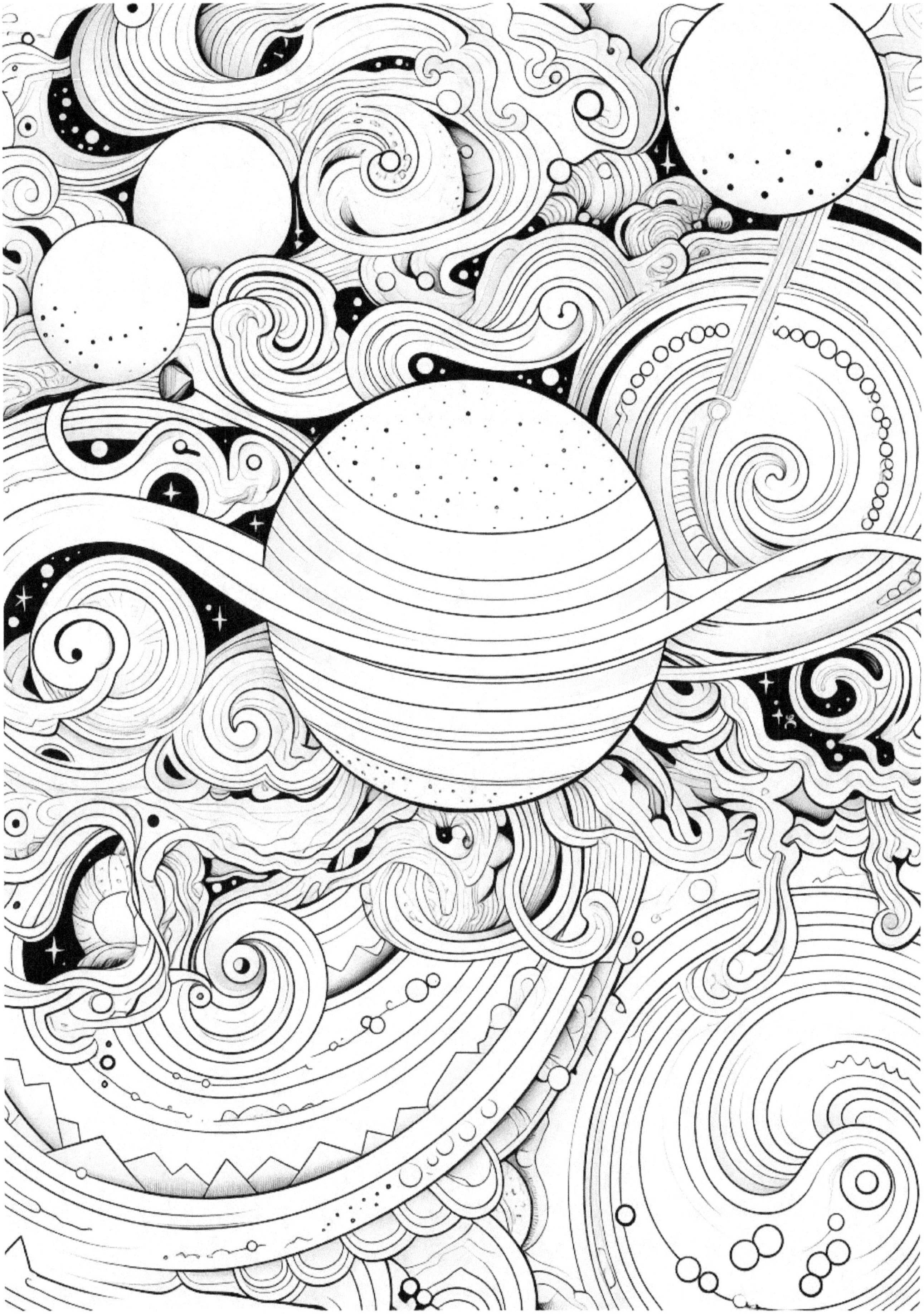

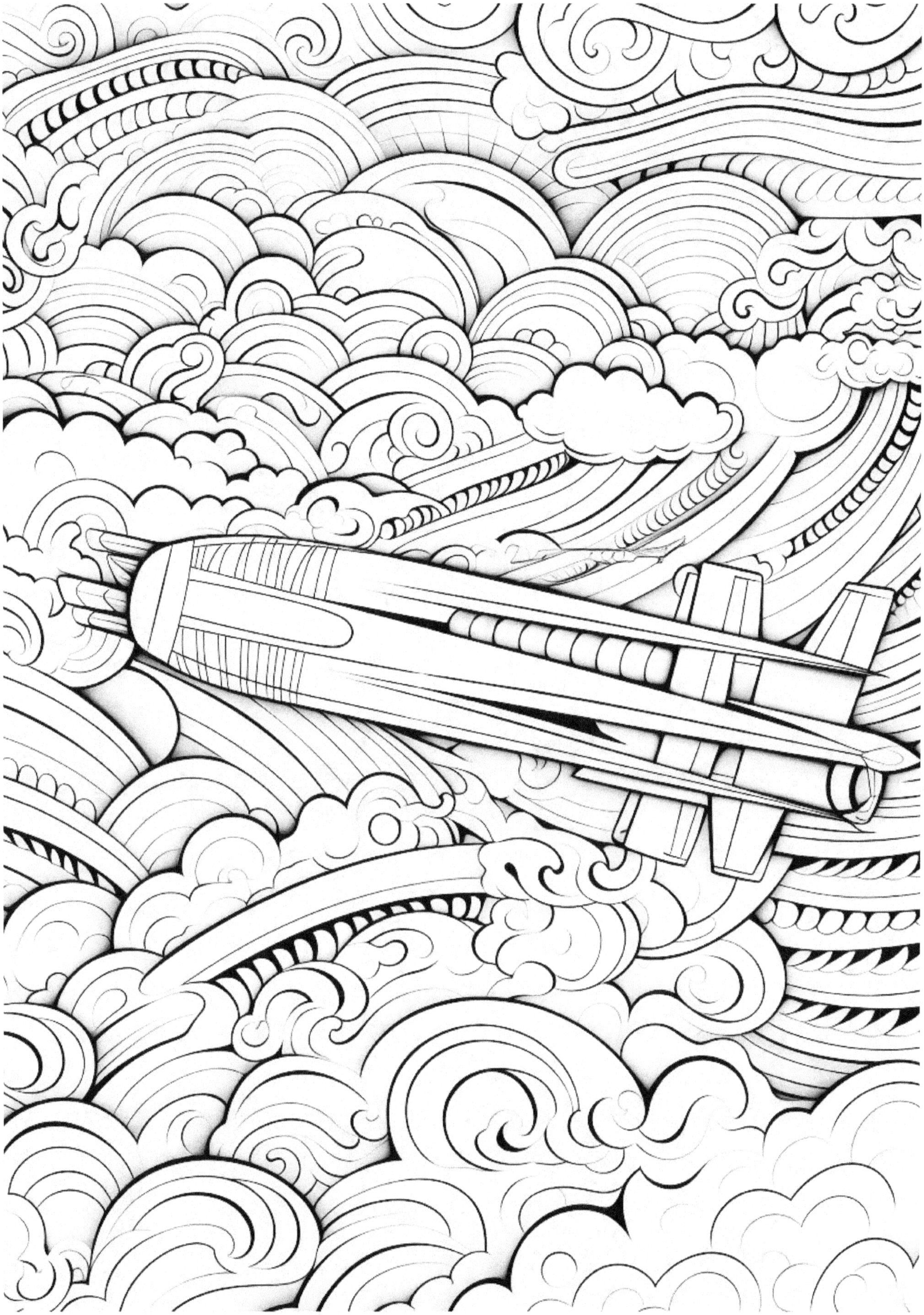

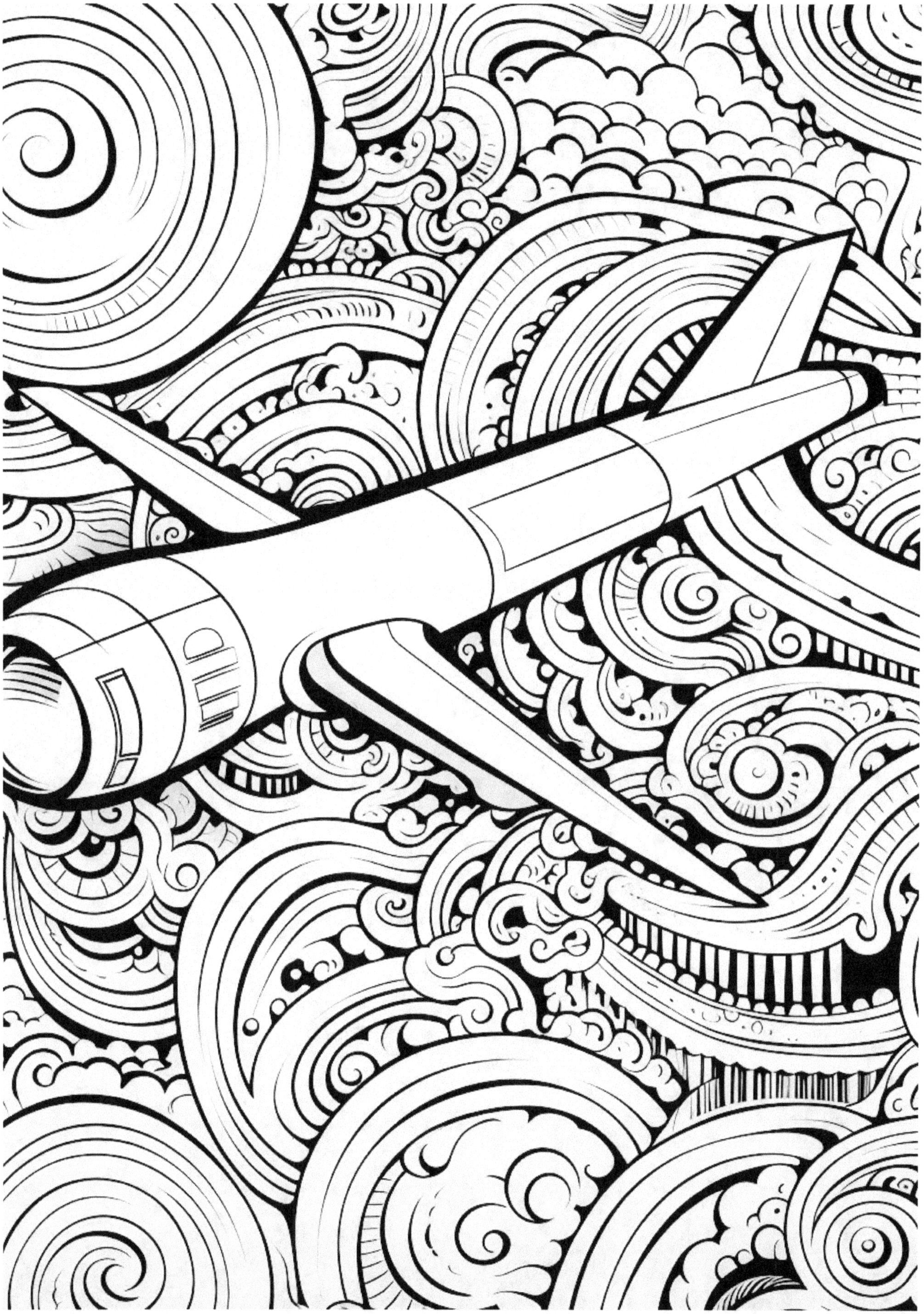

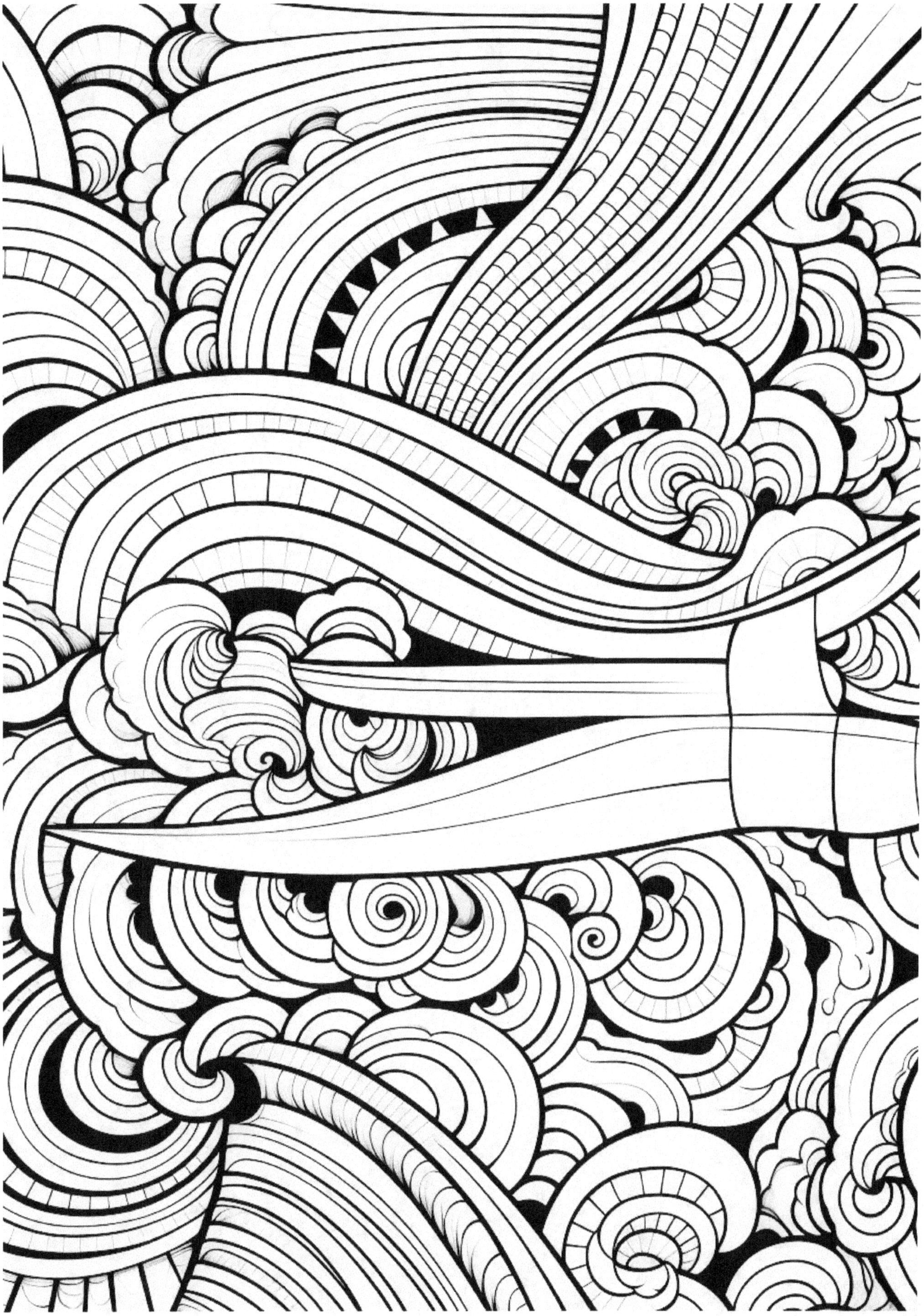

www.ingramcontent.com/pod-product-compliance
Lightning Source LLC
Chambersburg PA
CBHW082214290526
45794CB00009B/3542
* 9 7 9 8 8 6 4 3 3 3 4 1 9 *